PORTALS

*Energetic Doorways to Mystical
Experiences Between Worlds*

Enjoy these other books in the Common Sentience series:

AKASHA: *Spiritual Experiences of Accessing the Infinite Intelligence of Our Souls*

ANCESTORS: *Divine Remembrances of Lineage, Relations and Sacred Sites*

ANGELS: *Personal Encounters with Divine Beings of Light*

ANIMALS: *Personal Tales of Encounters with Spirit Animals*

ASCENSION: *Divine Stories of Awakening the Whole and Holy Being Within*

GODDESS: *Blessed Reunions with the Feminine Face of the Divine*

GODTALK: *Experiences of Humanity's Connections with a Higher Power*

GUIDES: *Mystical Connections to Soul Guides and Divine Teachers*

MEDITATION: *Intimate Experiences with the Divine through Contemplative Practices*

MEDIUMSHIP: *Sacred Communications with Loved Ones from Across the Veil*

NATURE: *Divine Experiences with Trees, Plants, Stones and Landscapes*

SHAMANISM: *Personal Quests of Communion with Nature and Creation*

SIGNS: *Sacred Encounters with Pathways, Turning Points, and Divine Guideposts*

SOUND: *Profound Experiences with Chanting, Toning, Music and Healing Frequencies*

WITCH: *Divine Alignments with the Primordial Energies of Magick and Cycles of Nature*

Learn more at sacredstories.com.

PORTALS

Energetic Doorways to Mystical
Experiences Between Worlds

FREDDY SILVA

SACRED STORIES
PUBLISHING

PORTALS: Energetic Doorways to Mystical Experiences Between Worlds

Freddy Silva

Print ISBN: 978-1-958921-58-6
EBook ISBN: 978-1-958921-59-3

Library of Congress Control Number: 2024932670

Published by Sacred Stories Publishing, Fort Lauderdale, FL USA

CONTENTS

PART THREE: INTERACTING WITH PORTALS

MEET THE SACRED STORYTELLERS
MEET THE AUTHOR

PART ONE

Understanding Portals

Once contact with the transcendent is lost,
existence in the world ceases to be possible.

— MIRCEA ELIADE

A PORTAL DEFINED

*I*t began innocently enough, as most magic does.

Over three decades ago. Eight o'clock at night.

Light drizzle falling, coating the ground like a gossamer of pearl. Typical weather on any given day in this corner of the planet.

The neophyte was instructed to find a stone, sit, be still, and connect with the spirit of place. He thought it an odd request. *How do I connect with a spirit of place? Do I pray? I thought religion had nothing to do with this type of work.*

Among the circle of upright megaliths, one appeared to be beckoning him. *Aren't stones supposed to be hard and lifeless objects? Am I imagining things?* But he did as instructed, sat on the damp grass, his back pressed to the cold bluestone. And closed his eyes.

The visions rushed in. A tall figure presented itself, humanlike but not quite human, luminous yet paradoxically physical. Two large, wing-like appendages wrapped around his back. With one arm extended, he handed the neophyte a sword sheathed in bluish flames. Some kind of non-verbal communication was exchanged, precisely what it meant was not immediately clear.

A sane mortal would have had the common sense to walk away by now, but the experience felt peaceful, even loving. He took a breath and immersed himself in this new, yet uncertain experience.

There's nothing like entering uncharted territory to shape one's character.

Then came a voice from above, quietly spoken. *In your own time, make your way over to the hut for a cup of tea.* One of the night watchmen had walked across the stone circle to remind the neophyte that private time had reached its conclusion. Time to depart. Or return, depending on one's point of view. *What? Has it been two hours? I couldn't have closed my eyes for more than a few minutes. What just happened?*

The neophyte stood up, groggy and uncertain, as though walking on shifting sand, and wandered over to the teacher. "So, how was it for you?" she said.

The neophyte calmly described his experience in vivid detail. It was unlike a dream or vision or hallucination, it seemed more like a meeting between two interpenetrating worlds where, for a few minutes—or two hours—two separate entities standing on opposite continents separated by time and space met on common ground.

No, none of this was chemically induced, he hadn't taken drugs.

The teacher was aghast. *You received a flaming sword on your first visit here? Oh dear. You've got your work cut out for you, young man.*

Indeed, from that moment forward, life would cease to be anything but dull. His sense of awareness expanded to accommodate a parallel reality, awakening a nascent memory that would gradually shape his life, his work, his spiritual outlook, even his perception of the universe as it is, rather than how it is perceived. All of this and more would reveal itself at his pace of development.

Has it really been three decades?

I know it has, I remember it as vividly as this morning because that neophyte was myself, and the account was my first conscious interaction with a portal—Stonehenge, no less.

If I am to write about portals, I do so from personal experience, and because I had no idea what they were or that they even existed. Or for that matter, that anything written from this point forward was even possible. I wouldn't change a single word or swap any experience for a wad of cash, because it has led me to where I am today: a teacher.

The word *portal* is thrown around today as casually as a cushion. Social media in particular is awash with posts by people believing they entered a portal just because sunlight caused a lens flare on the camera of their smartphone. Or they felt an unnerving presence while viewing a property. Or a tourist map marked the location of local portals that a fleet of Jeeps gladly took you to once you forked over a generous sum of money. It's not that straightforward. There are parameters that define a portal and how it shapes the experience of the individual with whom it interacts, while the experience itself is defined by what the individual is searching for, consciously or otherwise.

There are places on the land where the laws of physics, as we understand them, behave very differently. To those with their antennae extended, they feel like hotspots where the veil between worlds is thinner and the perception of overlapping realities is both apparent and immediate.

How is this possible? The human body is really nothing more than a conglomerate of atoms bound together by the laws of electricity, magnetism, and gravity. Not a very romantic image, I agree, yet it is the essence of what we are: a product of millions of pulsing and whirling pools of energy bound to each other, giving the illusion of one distinct organism. It is calculated that if all the air were expelled from a body, the entire mass of what constitutes it would occupy no more than a teaspoon.

A portal is governed by the same natural forces, invisible to the naked eye yet utterly real in its own level of reality—much like a radio station yet to be discovered further down the dial. A simple analogy is to compare a portal to a plank of wood. Sliding your hand along the fine, orderly grain, every so often it is interrupted by a knot where the living wood has grown around an obstruction. If it were visible to the naked eye, that's what a portal on the landscape would look like: an interruption, a vortex swirling in the smooth current of a river.

When a person's spatial awareness is duly engaged and mindful of its surroundings, these miniature universes become tangible and apparent. The more one interacts with this energy, the more it becomes visible in the mind's eye. And as one acclimates to this new reality, the experience gradually becomes second nature, an extension of the self, like learning to drive a car. Eventually, engaging with multiple places of power extends the body's electrical circuitry to the point where you become capable of observing energy with the naked eye. I've met people who can see the energy in color; one friend, an accomplished sound healer, can even hear the sound a portal generates.

Since the portal is an entry point of energy emanating from other realities, it becomes a stage for every player that ever existed, exists, or has yet to exist to cohabit a shared environment, be it for an instant or a lifetime.

Ancient traditions have much to say on the matter. They describe portals as resident places of the spirits, what scholars misinterpret as gods, although they're not far off the mark, since the traditional understanding of a god is a force of nature, the energy field or *soul* encompassing and inhabiting a drop of water, a blade of grass, a rock, an animal, or a person. To our predecessors and today's living shamans, portals assist the enlightenment of the individual by providing a more direct conduit to an astral reference library, or the means to communicate with other entities, be they alive or long since dissolved. And when used as places of power, portals are capable of storing information and directing it to where it needs to be applied.

Succinctly expressed, a portal is a supernatural opening in space and time connecting thoughts, dreams, and potentially objects and people with myriad points in the universe, even multiple levels of reality.

A portal is a contact station with the miraculous, an island of stability amid a landscape of chance.

Portals vary in size from the obscenely large (the Great Pyramid of Giza), to the very compact, such as the one in my apartment, which is three feet in diameter, and any dog entering the room will naturally gravitate toward it as though working a room to connect with a like-minded accomplice.

And despite their special locations throughout the landscape, portals are not as rare as one might think, nor are they always to be found among bucolic scenery or in the holiest room of an ancient temple. When I first moved to Portland, Maine, I went on a walkabout in this compact city to find its most active portals, to help myself acclimate with the spirit of place. I was able to locate five hotspots, all of them in parks, lawns, or places that had yet to succumb to development—an astonishing feat, given the speed of urbanization—except the one inside my apartment. My building appears to have been erected on an ancient Abenaki sacred site, and it attracts all kinds of spiritual people; a fifth site is partially visible amid the bay of islands at extreme low tide, thanks to an ocean on the rise. Together, they form a distinct shape, a mirror of the constellation Delphinus as it appeared above New England around 3000 B.C.

The city is now casually referred to as Portal-land.

So where are these portals? How do we find them? How did our predecessors work with them? How do they relate to ancient temples, sacred sites, and other places of power?

What practical benefit can they offer in this modern, disconnected century?

That's what this adventure is all about.

PORTALS AMONG THE ANCIENTS

———— 3†Ɛ ————

*B*eing intimately connected to the ways and rhythms of nature, our distant cousins were more attuned to the world around them, particularly its subtle landscape. Sensing and working with portals was a habit as common to them as shopping for a tin of baked beans is to us. Their practical and spiritual survival depended on it.

When working with something to that degree of intimacy, the elements become intertwined like vines to the point where discernment between what is physical and what is something else becomes irrelevant. Ancient Egyptians even coined a phrase for it: *as above so below.*

The relationship formed the cornerstone of sacred ritual and religion, but it also served a practical function. Since our predecessors regarded incarnation as a spiritual death, it was imperative to repair the severed umbilical cord with the subtle universe, reopen a connection and establish an advantage over this dominant, and often suffocating, physical domain.

And they went to great pains to achieve this connection. In northern New Mexico, it was customary for a tribesperson to climb the sacred mountain Tsé Bitʼaʼí to take part in a coming of age ceremony inside a sacred cave. Three days were spent in glorious isolation undertaking a vision quest to connect with the spirit of place, whereupon the individual was symbolically dismembered before being reconstituted and returned as a newborn individual.

Despite its seemingly gruesome nature, the ordeal served a vital function: to lessen the neophyte's tether to the physical world and allow their soul to become aware of its entrapment inside a limited vessel, thereby expanding its connection to the cosmos. With the ego relegated to the back seat and the soul in charge of the steering wheel, the individual became more aware of his or her purpose in life.

The fringe benefits were tremendous: expansion of latent psychic ability, the power of foresight, as well as the ability to shape the process of manifestation, within certain boundaries. Some people developed the ability to heal others or to interact with the weather, as recent events in the Amazon will attest when shamans were hired to end a long-standing drought. Torrential rain ensued within hours.

On a mountain that is a potent magnetic hotspot in its own right (Tsé Bit'a'í is the eroded throat of a prehistoric volcano), the location of the sacred cave contains the exact natural ingredients that amplify the electrical current flowing through the human body, which in turn activates the body's meridians and stimulates the pineal gland—all the required ingredients for a heightened state of consciousness.

For the Anasazi and Navajo, Tsé Bit'a'í was their portal.

The Tewa people of central New Mexico still perform a similar ritual on the summit of Tsikumu, another sacred hill that just happens to coincide with a geomagnetic hotspot. They refer to the inherent energy as *po-wa-ha*, which they say generates a portal into the Otherworld. The exact spot looks about as remarkable as a lump of concrete, marked by tumbledown stones, yet its power is palpable.

Indeed, some mountains are more sacred than others for this very reason. When you hear A-type mountain climbers describing, in mystic vocabulary, a sudden experience in the process of ascent, listen to them. One of my favorite accounts is by Maurice Herzog during his climb of Annapurna, a holy mountain in Nepal:

I had the strangest and most vivid impressions such as I had never before known in the mountains... all sense of exertion was gone, as though there was no longer any gravity... I had never seen such complete transparency, and I was living in a world of crystal. Sounds were indistinct. The atmosphere like cotton wool. An enormous gulf was between me and the world. This was a different universe... we were overstepping a boundary.

Climbers of Cadair Idris in Wales describe feelings of entering another reality, literally. Traditions highlight this specific mountain to be the main portal into Caer Annwn, the Gaelic Otherworld. There is no end of anecdotes of strangers walking toward the tarn below its summit and feeling the presence of two large hounds, the black dogs who serve as guides while the soul fumbles in the dark and acclimates to its new and unsure domain.

Like many of its kind, Cadair Idris is a geomagnetic hotspot that coincides with a gravitational anomaly, generating the kind of energy that stimulates human passage from the known into the unknown. Most climbers are not consciously aware of this interaction, and it is probably for this reason that a legend was devised as a mnemonic, reminding visitors of the supernatural potential in this mountain. It tells of a water dragon who was bound to the lake until Arf Fawr worked his magic on the creature and set it loose. Those brave enough to spend the night will awaken as a poet, a madman, or a corpse.

Deciphering this symbolic language, the dragon represents the meandering nature of energy whose power is directed by the individual's own disposition, which in turn defines the outcome.

The relationship between naturally occurring energy vortices and mountains explains why so many mountain shrines and temples were placed in architecturally irrational and, frankly, dangerous places. They represent the X that marks the spot, the portal as umbilical cord to a higher frequency.

The holiest mountain in China, Hua Shan, is one such example. To reach the shrine near the summit, it is necessary to walk across a vertical chasm while holding onto a simple chain bolted to the cliff face, with nothing but air separating you from an unyielding surface 6,000 feet below. It is perhaps the most dangerous pilgrimage route on the planet, a one way avenue for daredevils and madwomen attempting to defy death just to discover life. To deter casual visitors, the mountain was given the nickname *number one steepest mountain under heaven*, yet none of this deters those seeking immortality, or the plethora of medicinal plants and drugs to be found along the way.

What drives ten of thousands of people to this portal is its long association with transcendence. The crazy climbers of Hua Shan are typically followers of one of the oldest spiritual practices in the Far East, *Tao*, specifically the development of *xian*, whereby a person attains immortality by means of supernatural abilities developed as a result of contact with heavenly realms, either through spiritual self-cultivation or immersion with special places on the land.

Tao first arrived in Japan around 8000 B.C. as *Tayi*, *The Way of the Gods*. Also referred to simply as *The Way*, it encompasses seventeen teachings introduced by two gods after a global flood devastated the Earth. The doctrine of *Tayi* attempts to define the undefinable: the ebb and flow of energy that underlies the natural order of the universe and of reality itself. Although its qualities are ineffable, this subtle force is discernible by practitioners of mindfulness, who claim that proper relationship with the forces underpinning a portal awakens the Great Human within. Given such unparalleled benefits, it is not surprising that *Tayi* became the foundation of Shinto, Japan's oldest religion, whose members, the Gentlemen of the Way, climb Mt. Fuji-yama as part of their ritual *to enter the mountain* and reach the paradisal state of the Otherworld.

This spiritual ideal was interpreted literally by the time it reached southern Britain. Barely tethered to the weather-beaten coast of Cornwall, the island of Tintagel has long been associated with vision quests and magic, and specifically with the exploits of Arth-Gwr and Merdyn, otherwise known as Arthur and Merlin.

The island has a hollow interior and was once a source of high quality gems and crystals. In essence, it is a giant geode. Access is via Merdyn's cave, a natural, dark passage that runs at sea level through the entire base of the island. The passage once served as the starting point of an initiation ritual, whereby the candidate spent the night huddling among slippery rocks, attacked from both sides by the loud thrashing from a feisty incoming tide, forcing them to face fear and, hopefully, control it.

If successful (meaning they hadn't drowned), the candidate ascended into the belly of the island via a conduit in the roof. Settled inside this womb-like environment, he or she connected with the portal and journeyed to faraway worlds for several days before climbing up a natural tube resembling an umbilical cord, to emerge gratefully at the summit of Tintagel. At this point the individual, still groggy from an out-of-body odyssey, was taken to an outcrop where a *telluric current*—science jargon for a pathway of earth energy—flows toward the mainland and a church dedicated to Madryn, the mother of the Gaelic gods. The exact spot is marked by a carving on the bedrock in the shape of a footprint, into which the person placed their foot and was declared *risen*.

It would take until the late twentieth century before modern technology recognized the entire island as one giant geomagnetic anomaly, hence why it was chosen above all other, more suitable nearby locations.

Such traditions are part and parcel of the process of initiation, which means *to become conscious*. And they are culturally shared throughout the world. The two prominent geomagnetic hotspots in Portugal happen to coincide with the regions' two most sacred mountains, and its oldest and most concentrated chthonic centers: Monsanto—literally *sacred mountain*—and Sintra, named for the Sumerian lunar goddess Sin. Thus, if you honored the Moon, you were technically a *sinner*, or so the Catholic church would have you believe. On these two mountains, you will come across wondrous and remote temples, shrines, and hermitages dedicated to isolation and the total absorption of the Divine. There are hermit caves, dolmens (a group of standing stones supporting a capstone), even rock-cut graves that are too shallow for preserving a dead body, but very practical for temporary shamanic travel.

When the energy hotspot remains unadulterated, a sacred mountain requires no human embellishment, its portal is palpable even to the casual traveler, particularly if its energy is enhanced over long periods of time by the devotion of practitioners in a spiritual community. Arunachala in India is a prime example. Like many of its kind, Arunachala is rich in traditions of interaction between otherworldly beings with humans, and as such, illustrates the very purpose of the portal as a place where ideas are exchanged between worlds.

It is interesting to note that in the mystical traditions of Persia, Japan, and the lands of the Hopi, sacred mountains are seen as meeting places between heaven and earth. Skeptics might see nothing magical in this because, to them, a mountain is physically the closest point to the sky, in which case *all* mountains would be sacred. Yet they are not. There is an important distinction insofar as these cultures describe the exact location of the sacred cave, shrine, or ritual center as being connected to the sky by a luminous tube or hollow reed along which the spirit of the initiate travels outward, and conversely, the energy of a spirit or a god descends. For the Hopi this conduit is the *sipapu* reed, for Persians it is the *reed of heaven*.

Perhaps the least known and certainly most perceivable sacred mountain portal is that of Kura Tawhiti in New Zealand. Twelve thousand years ago, it was a landscape temple for starwalkers called Urukehu: unusually tall, light-skinned, and red-haired gods who regularly sailed across the Pacific Ocean to Lake Titicaca, Easter Island, and New Zealand in large, double-hulled canoes. After a swarm of meteorites hit the Earth and generated a global flood in 9700 B.C., the surviving Urukehu intermarried with the indigenous people of Easter Island, the Waitaha, whose progeny live in small numbers in New Zealand today.

I was not aware of this tribal tradition when I first hiked the two hours to reach Kura Tawhiti, nor did I know very much of the latent power of the portal in this breathtaking corner of the planet. Along the ridge toward the summit, a colossal limestone monolith was shaped with stone mauls to portray the face of the tutelary goddess Marotini.

Kura Tawhiti, along with two more landscape temples across the valley, constitute the Birthplace of the Gods.

Sitting at the base of Marotini, I still recall recording, in my memory, a ream of information issuing from this hotspot that would become the foundation for my sixth book. The download was as clear as watching a movie. If you doubt your psychic ability, an interaction with Marotini will remove it. Free from human folly, the energy at this location is as pure and unadulterated as it gets.

And yet this is not the only portal at this astral academy. Walking further along the ridge, two massive boulders resembling sentinel dogs appeared to be guarding something of great value. The untrained eye will see nothing around but wild grass and rock. Going with the flow, I was guided to a spot between the two suggestive boulders to a slab lying just beneath the thin cover of soil. As I stood on this platform, a kind of screen appeared in front of me revealing a glacial landscape from long ago, with trees covering the now barren terrain and unusual mammals, long since extinct, scampering down the slopes of adjacent mountains. For minutes—I don't recall how long, one loses track of time at these places—I was immersed in the dual reality of a portal while it communicated information which, little did I know at the time, would feed my work in years to come. Not surprisingly, each time I travel to New Zealand, I visit Kura Tawhiti to collect more messages.

TRAVELING IN TIME

Speaking of time, for a number of years, a local antiquarian in southern Wales has been walking up Cairn Ingli to collect incidences of missing time. The name means *hill of angels*. It is located not far from the outcrop that produced the bluestones that would be dragged 140 miles across mountains, vales, rivers, and forests, and placed upright on a plain and named Stonehenge.

The immediate region around Cairn Ingli is rife with references to otherworldly domains, electromagnetic anomalies, granite outcrops where the Earth's magnetic field points south, balls of light, faeries, and of course, disturbances in the time continuum. By definition, a portal involves that little understood phenomenon called *gravity*. What *is* understood is that gravity is not constant, and its fluctuations affect the flow of time, or at least our perception of it.

The antiquarian in question has amassed hundreds of cases where visitors to Cairn Ingli descend the hill and voluntarily complain of having experienced missing time. Obviously, such anecdotes fail every scientific protocol by a long yard, yet the gentleman calculated that the experiences tended to cluster around specific times of day: just prior to sunrise, eleven thirty in the morning, and less often, between two and three in the morning, although people rarely climb a mountain in the middle of the night. The next phase of his research involved synchronized watches. Leaving one at the base and giving the other to any person hiking the hill, when the timepieces were reunited and compared, anywhere from five to twenty minutes differed between them.

Incidentally, the same phenomenon occurs inside genuine crop circles which, unlike human hoaxes, are created using a combination of electromagnetism, the bending of gravity, and sound. And inside these geometric masterpieces, people experience the same states of elation as they do on sacred mountains.

Crop circles are the portals of our era.

THE MEMORY OF PLACE

Some of the most lucid descriptions of working with portals comes from Australian aboriginal tribes living among featureless terrain, who are able to accurately find their way around by sensing invisible lines of force called *djalkiri*. When tribespeople walk across these spirit roads, they hear the frequency imprinted by those who walked before. In a way, the *djalkiri* behave like strips of magnetic tape, recording the resonance of every individual to the point where entire conversations can be replayed. Such dreaming tracks are imprinted with a permanent record of events, enabling tribespeople to walk great distances while listening to a data stream. And just like modern day cloud computing, the information can be accessed on demand, if you know how.

The *djalkiri* lead to spiritually important locations, despite two points being physically separated by hundreds of miles of desert. A scientific study found that when these spirit roads are used to figure out directions to non sacred places, the margin of error is as high as 67 percent. But when using them to access sacred places, the error is less than 3 percent.

Aboriginals have long used such energy pathways to locate their portals. Standing in these invisible doorways, they're able to telepathically transmit information that is received as an image by another person meditating in a similar portal some distance away.

Why waste money on a smartphone when you can access this subtle energy for free, with a clear signal to boot.

In parts of Africa—Kenya in particular—portals are referred to as *baraka*. In Arizona, the Hopi call them *spots of the fawn,* and the origin of the phrase comes with a particularly vivid description of the creation of the world. When the Creator chose to make the Earth, It sent a tribesman to the South Pole with a drum—as one does when walking in temperatures of minus eighty degrees. As the tribesman heard the heartbeat of the Earth, he beat a sympathetic rhythm on his drum, at which moment the Earth became abundant with all forms of life. However, some places became more potent than others, and those became the *spots of the fawn.*

In Central America, the demarcation between sacred and profane space often appears in local legends. Using allegorical language, a story will convey the purpose of place to anyone who decodes its symbolism, thereby protecting a spiritual location or concept from abuse.

The Maya Otherworld is called *Xibalba (firestone with the power to transform).* It is regarded as a land of plenty, reachable either during ritual or when the soul inevitably departs from its fleshy vessel for good. At the center of *Xibalba* stands a mighty world tree, an *axis mundi* from which all knowledge emanates. Maya wisdom-keepers sought natural hotspots where this tree of knowledge pierces all tiers of existence, directing the energy to travel to the Otherworld and gain access to deities, ancestors, celestial forces, even the knowledge of eternity. Furthermore, shamans were capable of opening this communication between two worlds via an elaborate ritual that dissolved any limitation imposed on the body, empowering them to divine the future and allow the power of the supernatural to flow into their daily activities. Such locations were generally referred to as *bridal chambers* because, when a person successfully reached the Otherworld and returned, they were said to have consummated a marriage with a Divine bride, a woman who embodies the sum of all existing knowledge.

This Mayan world tree, *Wacah Chan,* can be seen inside Balam-ka-ànché, a sacred cave in Yucatan. The tree's meandering roots, trunk, limbs, and canopy were created from the slow percolation of water in limestone over the course of millennia until an impressive stalagmite was formed that seems to hold up the ceiling of the cave. In this dark, damp, subterranean world, countless initiates came to experience *Xibalba*, perhaps choosing this cave over thousands like it precisely because its water sculpted passages to resemble a female vulva and its fallopian tubes.

One literally enters the womb of a Divine woman.

That this specific cave was used as a bridal chamber is immortalized in a local legend which tells of a young man who wished to marry a young maiden, against the wishes of her mother, so he hid his beloved bride inside the cave, thus the origin of its alternative name, *Xtacumbi*, the *hidden lady*.

Inside its sensory deprived world, the soul comes to tangle with supernatural beings and pick the fruits of the tree of knowledge. Ledges cut long ago around *Wacah Chan* still hold dozens of small clay vessels once filled with offerings to the spirit world, as well as incense and narcotics to help ease the passage of the soul from the body and into the Otherworld.

No wonder ancient cultures describe portals as *increase centers*, where the correct use of ritual elicits a life force that intensifies the vitality of the individual and, when directed through intent, the vitality of the land itself. This relationship is evident in the way the most ancient habitation clusters or conurbations grew outward from a seed, such as a standing stone or a shrine that marked, protected, and maintained the integrity of the portal.

It worked for our ancestors, and it works just as well for us.

WHEN PORTALS
BECAME TEMPLES
——— 3†Ɛ ———

*a*ncient people developed a keen affinity for the land and rarely, if ever, required a physical structure to show them the location of a portal. They could sense it. Those with highly developed perception could see the fluid motion of invisible currents wandering across mountains, rivers, and fields. Adding rocks, sticks, or a mound of soil to what was perfectly obvious was redundant. Besides, since this energy is influenced by the motions of the Earth and Moon, subjected to the daily gravitational push-pull of the Sun, and the whims of the geomagnetic field, it shifts from place to place over time, adapting to the ebb and flow of nature, much like a nomad migrates towards the equator in winter and returns to the pole in summer.

On Earth, where change is the only constant, it is unrealistic to assume the relationship between humans and portals would remain unchanged forever. Major upheavals in climate between 5000 and 1300 B.C. brought incremental disruption to society's doorstep, and with it the need to adapt. Perhaps the most direct transformation was humanity's gradual detachment from nature and distancing from the supernatural. As we gradually lost the ability to sense those special places on the land, something needed to be done to direct people to *the spots of the fawn*.

The remedy was to superimpose portals with manmade structures, providing future generations with readily identifiable markers. Stone circles, menhirs (standing stones), dolmens, pyramids, stupas, passage mounds—we literally went on a binge of temple building around the world. That temples and other sacred places were not located haphazardly is evidenced in the *Building Texts*, an Egyptian account detailing the arrival of gods along the Nile who sited temples *at carefully chosen locations*. These unusual people not only possessed the gift of sensing the laws of nature, they were also capable of manipulating them. The text emphasizes the replenishing and enhancement of telluric energy before housing it inside a permanent structure. And just like that, portals that once had stood in open nature were now defined and protected within specially designed environments.

Temples became meeting points between gods and mortals, places for mystical revelation and reconnection with realities beyond our own. As self-help centers, they could offer healing and guidance on-demand, early precursors to the Samaritans. In times of chaos, when people lost their rudder, their compass pointed south, and the signal-to-noise ratio deteriorated, the temple became a stabilizing commodity. The Maya were succinct on this point when they stated how the temple exists *to transform the individual into a god, into a bright star*. Every action on sacred ground was performed with the intention of raising the individual into a force of nature, to the status of a god.

As Egyptian priests remarked in the temple of Edfu, *We will continue building temples until people recognize they are the temple*, to which they added an inscription: *The temple shall act as a magical protector for you, in heaven and in earth, unfailingly and regularly and eternally*. And they were right, for nothing is more powerful than a person in regular contact with the cosmos. Instead of playing the game of life holding four cards, you deal from a full deck.

However, no matter how much magic exists in these sacred places, they are not vending machines dispensing instant enlightenment. Like any functional partnership, you have to offer a little of yourself, meet the temple halfway. Then be careful what you ask for, you might just receive it.

THE TEMPLE AND YOU

They say nothing beats personal experience, and I agree. All this research makes for great storytelling in books and documentaries, and yet when I began fully engaging with ancient sacred places and other portals, I had no idea just how powerful the interaction could be, not to mention the quality of information one is able to retrieve.

It has certainly made writing much easier.

My passion for the temples of the Andes began when I was six, after reading *Prisoners of the Sun*, one of a series of classic graphic books by one of my heroes, Georges Remi. Yet it took until I was in my fifties before I felt confident enough to handle the intensity of Andean power places. It worked out so well that I subsequently led many tours there.

Peru and Bolivia have, in my experience, some of the most potent portals on the planet—particularly those scattered throughout the high Andes, where the energy is raw and unfiltered. It is not everyone's bag of coca leaf, one can either handle it from the outset or develop an affinity over time by first attempting gentler sites elsewhere and allowing the interaction to raise your vibration. Like taking a hairdryer to a foreign country, a 110-volt appliance plugged into a 240-volt socket will not end well for the appliance.

Eight hundred feet above Cuzco lies the sprawling, megalithic complex of Saqsayhuaman. Half of its cyclopean masonry was pulled down and shoved downhill by the Spanish to build the city, yet what remains is still breathtaking. Stones as tall as nineteen feet appear to have been softened by intense heat and shaped to fit around each other without mortar, using as many as sixteen angles.

On the lower layer of a serrated wall resembling the wing of a falcon, there's a spot marked by a stone of such presence that you feel pulled toward it as though caught in a fast moving current. I even referred to it as "a portal stone" the first time I saw it from the summit of the hill opposite.

The effect increases in intensity as you approach. As I launched into a lengthy explanation of the site for my group, it became obvious I was struggling to maintain focus, as though someone was distracting me by whispering in my ear. And no, it was not the result of chewing coca leaf. That's precisely what was happening: a voice *was* giving me information about the site, really juicy stuff, things no one had ever taken into consideration about *sexy-woman* (as the local guides pronounce it for tourists). Grappling with two parallel worlds, I wrapped up my discombobulated monologue and waved off the group to go experience the site.

I took out my notebook and wrote down what I'd heard before I forgot it. After a month of research, the information transmitted turned out to be right on track. Thank you, spirit of place.

Perhaps the altitude accounts for the potency of Andean portals. When combined with certain mineral properties in the stone, it generates hotspots of profound intensity. A long walk from Saqsayhuaman takes you to Amaru Marka Wasi, the *house of the serpent*. Two adjacent manmade caves have been cut into an outcrop of andesite, each marking the flow of masculine and feminine telluric currents. Since these currents behave like serpents, the given name aptly describes the function of the site. Meditating in either cave is an intense experience, even for a few minutes, as each current is amplified by a ceramic glaze composed of magnesium, silica, and aluminium coated on the cave wall. What motivated the creators of these repositories of earth energy to add this exotic mixture to an already powerful place? It's a mystery.

I walked around the perimeter of the site with my Aymara co-guide Edgar, admiring outcrops of rock shaped into steps that lead nowhere, curving basins, and other oddities. Walking beside a square alcove cut into the stone, we stopped as though barred by an invisible arm, looked at each other and smiled in agreement as if to say, *I sense it too, let's do ceremony here.* And we did. The alcove is deliberately shaped in the ratio 6:5, a minor third in music; together with the chemical composition of the stone, it makes for excellent acoustics in an open environment. The combination was intense. Every participant was visibly altered by the experience.

Andean temple builders, I've observed, were prodigious when it also came to marking portals with what can only be described as doorways leading nowhere into the faces of rocks or hills. Near the shore of Lake Titicaca—altitude 12,500 feet—a false door carved in the shape of a T marks a portal called Amaru Muru, a vertical sandstone hill brimming with iron. The name translates as *white bearded man of Mu*, and the site has been sacred to the Aymara for as long as the tribe can remember.

Local villagers grant this portal great respect and prefer to give it a wide berth, in fact, they loathe to approach it, particularly when the sun is close to setting. When Catholic missionaries arrived, they went so far as to call it the Devil's Gate, although they were apt to award such names to any place that was sacred to everyone else. Edgar was looking uncharacteristically apprehensive as he concluded a shamanic ceremony for my group. *I sense it too*, I whispered, and suggested we return in the morning, but I also felt the need to experience this discomfort so I could write about it. As I pressed my forehead to the warm stone, I could clearly see a red, laser-like point of light approaching head-on, a glowing beam drilling between my eyes, had I allowed it. I felt a sensation of being pulled into the T-shaped doorway, instinctively pulled back, and rubbed my aching forehead.

I would later learn how one individual had been physically sucked into the portal, reappearing a few days later, dazed and confused. Whether this story is true or not, local villagers often describe a blue light glowing from within, and oddly dressed people walking out of the portal and towards Lake Titicaca.

Amaru Muru was deliberately carved to match the rising of Venus before the sunrise on the spring equinox, an alignment that is unique to sites around the world associated with initiation. Clearly, the site was understood for what it was in its natural form and had been physically marked to identify it as a place of ritual. We returned in the morning to find the energy of the place clean and welcoming, in total contrast to the evening before. We walked around the hill to the rear of the portal to find a physical tunnel where once a young and curious Edgar had slid down by accident, only to arrive at a village ten kilometres away. The villagers chastised him for being foolish, for it could have turned out worse: had he slid down the other tunnel, he'd have ended up 400 miles away in Cuzco.

The Andes is full of amazing sites. Perhaps the most dramatic is Naupa Huaca, a manmade cave burrowed into a steep ravine. The short yet demanding, near vertical hike is worth the effort to see a horizontal false door with a niche carved with laser-like precision from a rare outcrop of bluestone. Containing high amounts of magnetite and generating an audible timbre when struck, it is the same material from which the smaller megaliths of Stonehenge in England were fashioned. Its seclusion in a steep valley 9,800 feet above sea level, together with the electromagnetic currents flowing through the portal, plus the sonic and magnetic qualities of the stone, demonstrate how the architect went to a lot of trouble to source these qualities, least of all because they make Naupa Huaca an ideal location for a thorough bodily adjustment.

It's not by accident the locals refer to this as a *spirit door* or *window into paradise*, qualities inherent in the chosen name: a *naupa* refers to an inhabitant of the spirit world. We have performed ceremonies here for years and rarely does anyone leave without being transformed on some level after kneeling inside the portal. It takes a hard heart to stand here and not feel the palpable energy of place. It is transfixing as much as it is bewitching.

ENERGY MARKERS MADE OF STONE

Anyone who travels the British Isles cannot be but impressed by the sheer number of sacred places packed into a relatively small territory. They come in all shapes and sizes and qualities: standing stones, stone circles, passage mounds, and dolmens. In time, many such temples and the portals they protect were supplanted by humble Celtic chapels, which in turn were superseded by those gracious portals of the medieval era, the gothic cathedrals.

Like the Andean sites, the rudimentary temples in Cornwall and Wales are close to the bone. Unlike the Andean sites, they are more affable, possibly because they were erected later in history and as such carry less of the burden of time, and probably because many continue to be maintained by an army of people who appreciate the old traditions.

The area around Maenclochog—where the bluestones for Stonehenge were quarried—has a fair number of menhirs acting as markers of portals. In my experience, the most potent tend to lie off the beaten track, on an obscure promontory or forgotten footpath, many requiring decent map-reading skills to reach. An hour walking through dramatic hills along rarely trodden paths to find a twelve-foot-tall stone is an adventure in itself, least of all because the sense of remote accomplishment makes it personal: you made the effort to source your very own monolith.

In addition to the solitude, a rarely visited site presents another advantage over overtly advertised places. Since menhirs are placed on vortices of energy, the very composition of the stone absorbs energy like a battery stores an electrical charge, and that charge needs to be grounded from time to time. In hindsight I wish someone had instructed me on this fine point when I was learning my craft, because the moment I came across my personal menhir, I exclaimed to my colleague, *It hasn't talked to anyone for ages, it feels like it has something to say.* As I stretched my arm to touch the damp granite, what felt like a hand pulled mine towards the stone, to which I became permanently attached. I don't recall much of the next twenty-four hours except being depleted of energy, driven back to the cottage where we were staying, and sleeping until the following afternoon.

I finally awoke, showered, and went downstairs; my colleague was sitting in the garden waiting to hear of my experience. I couldn't stop speed talking for two hours, regurgitating what the stone had shown me, because I was able to freeze frame every image like a strip of film and describe in painstaking detail everything it had experienced for hundreds of years: marriages, baptisms, duels, deaths, it all came pouring out. The lonely old stone had stored the energy of each encounter and, like a good neighbor, conveyed the gossip to the first hapless visitor whose touch grounded its energy.

Although an experience I'd rather not relive, it did serve a useful purpose for someone who'd later write about it.

Dowsers report similar incidents. An army colonel took up the practice as a distraction during retirement, only to become one of the foremost practitioners in Britain. Because of his military training, his power of concentration was the best it could be, and he was not prone to fancy, nor did he judge the outcome, he merely observed with detachment, which is the correct attitude to adopt when sensing the unseen.

Like me, Colonel Thomas was fascinated by the energy and simplicity of manmade stone monuments in Wales. On one notable occasion, he dowsed a strong energy field emanating from a menhir and allowed his curiosity to get the better of him. As he reached out to touch the stone, the static electricity sent him flying for several feet before landing on his pride. It took another twenty minutes before feeling returned to his forearm and fingers. I'm certain he, too, would prefer not to relive the experience.

By contrast, Avebury stone circle in England is a gentle temple, a site of feminine energy, which is a characteristic common to lunar sites. Up until the arrival of Puritan zealots, most of its 143 stones were still intact and collectively acted as markers for the motions of the moon. Seen from above, a massive ring of stones contained two smaller circles and resembled two fried eggs in a skillet.

Having lived nearby for five years, I could come and go at any time of day without being disturbed, particularly at night or dawn. Every visit has taught me something new, and hundreds of encounters later, it still delivers no end of surprises. In addition to being a giant calculator, each stone is individual, each naturally shaped and chosen to represent a concept, quality or teaching, making the original scouting for material an arduous chore in itself. Of the two entry stones, one resembles a male fist holding an invisible sword—and indeed marks the flow of a masculine telluric current—while its counterpart resembles a pregnant earth mother and marks the flow of a female current. Together, they form a definitive doorway.

The genius of this temple is how each stone serving a practical function is placed over a natural vortex of upwelling energy, what is known as a *blind spring,* which in turn is transmitted to the stone. One such megalith is renown in local folklore as a place of healing. It features a natural seat where the afflicted sits, above which a hollow tube in the stone allows a healer to tone with the voice or a musical instrument. The acoustic resonance generated is profound and, coupled with the energy upwelling, generates an environment that promotes wellness. It is one of the earliest surviving examples of sound healing. Naturally, it was named the Devil's Chair.

Another stone of note resembles a stump, having been decapitated by religious fanatics. Placed above another vortex, it originally featured a hole through which a marrying couple would slide their hands to perform the Gaelic handfasting ceremony. It is still used in wedding ceremonies today, as British law once again recognizes so-called pagan marriages.

PORTALS OF THE FAR NORTH

The remote archipelago of Outer Hebrides, off the western coast of Scotland, is about as far as one can get away from crowds to experience some of the best preserved stone circles in Europe. Protected by layers of peat and generally unscathed by human folly, they provide an idea of what it is like to engage with sacred space in the way it was designed to be. The region around Callanais is particularly packed with them, and if you're prepared to read a map and pack a sturdy pair of waterproof boots, then you will be treated to serenity and the luxury of an empty stone circle.

Taking the only road south, blink and you will miss Ceann Hulavig, whose thin monoliths breach the brow of the hill for a few seconds as though its architect had the foresight to render it invisible to frivolous tourists. The angular slabs of schist are covered with pale green, hoary lichen-like blankets against the bitter northerly wind. The view of undulating lands and lochs uncontaminated by modern sprawl are a bonus in any type of weather. It is a site designed for vision quests, and anyone who stands with their back to the stones is immediately transported to another horizon in no time at all. It is effortless to leave the body here, to the point where it is imperative to have another person detach you from your stone and remind you the last airplane off the island leaves in an hour.

Given such an effect, I was hardly astonished to later discover its original name means *the room of seeing*.

Undoubtedly, the focal point is Callanais itself. A series of avenues in the shape of a cross with a ring of thirteen sinuous monoliths in the middle, the stones of Callanais are designed to mark the passage of the Moon's most southerly trajectory across a southern horizon of mountains resembling the body of a woman. Every 18.6 years, a visitor from this vantage point observes the orb rising out of the belly of Cailleach na Mointeach (Old Woman of the Moors), tracking as it barely skims across her sleeping body before setting into the vessel that is the Clisham range to the west. Seen from the avenue of stones, the Moon makes a spectacular sight as it descends behind a natural outcrop beyond the stone circle, only to reappear beside its central and tallest monolith, a sinuous piece of gneiss measuring 19.6 feet. The interaction between landscape and manmade temple demonstrates the inseparable bond between ground and sky.

Callanais is a place for introspection and dreaming as well as retrieval of information. It is possible, under the correct circumstances, to get a lot of personal work done there. The dramatic uprights forming the central circle became the meeting place for wisdom-keepers more than 5,000 years ago, a tradition later maintained by the Druidhe.

At some stage in its organic development, Callanais gained a restricted chamber in the form of an earthen passage mound pointing to the spring equinox. The chamber acts as a concentrator of the telluric current flowing through the site to generate the conditions for journeying, much like the sacred cave of the Navajo.

As a group, the Callanish stone circles are fed by the energetic properties that congregate specifically at this location, for they cluster within an extremely strong gravity anomaly zone, while the locations of the circles themselves delineate a localized region of low natural magnetism. It is one of the best surviving examples of giving visible expression to a portal.

A similar methodology is at play off the northern Scottish coast, in the Orkney archipelago, as though the region's temple builders were borrowing from the same manual. The Ring of Brodgar was placed with its center marking a fault line, while downhill, the Stenness circle is located precisely at the branching of two fault lines. In essence, the quartz rich stones are in a permanent state of subtle vibration that, in turn, generates a piezoelectric effect. It follows a distinct pattern throughout the world of sacred sites being strategically located to take advantage of such anomalies, the idea being to generate an environment that influences a visitor's state of consciousness.

The stones themselves were carefully considered to amplify these relationships, hence the reason why they were often sourced far from their intended positions. The stones at Callanais, for example, contain a high concentration of hornblende, a silicate of iron, transforming them into lighting rods that attract electric and magnetic currents to the site—and, on occasion, lightning.

GATEWAYS TO ORION?

In Japan, the traditional approach to a portal is marked by a gateway made from two wooden poles connected by a rope stretched between them. In time, the rope was replaced with a wooden crosspiece extending beyond the poles and the whole structure painted in cinnabar red, the color of the Otherworld, just as it is on the opposite side of the Pacific in the land of the Maya. The *torri* arch represents the gate to the abode of *kami*, the nature spirits in the Far East. And of physical gods, too, for any person who exemplified the qualities of the unseen was awarded the status of god.

What is unusual about the *torri* is how they depict a specific location in the sky: the poles represent the lower body of the Orion constellation, the crosspiece its Belt stars. But it's the space in-between that is significant, the area where humans pass, for it is called *Heart of the Sky*, which refers to a nebula poetically named M42 in that region of Orion. This cluster of stars and gasses is said to be a true portal, the location from where the gods originated. It is a view shared by other cultures, especially the Maya, who additionally point out it is the source of all life itself, once the point of origin for humans. The concept is so central to Mayan belief that hearths in temples and traditional homes are marked with three stones, each representing the ubiquitous Belt stars. It would take until the invention of the Hubble Space Telescope for science to recognize M42 as the biggest star forming region of the galaxy.

How did our ancestors know this?

Whether by design or necessity, the *torri* evolved into the dolmen, that ubiquitous monument composed of upright stones balancing a huge capstone weighing as much as 140 tons. They are elegant structures in themselves, even though originally covered by mounds of earth that rainfall gradually removed, leaving behind the stone interior. The design originated in the Korean peninsula, where the greatest concentration still exists. Dolmen is a Korean term whose approximate translation is *stone of the shaman*.

The design was exported westward to India, and from there to the Mediterranean, Portugal, Denmark and France, before reaching Ireland and Scotland. Of 80 percent that have been excavated, fewer than 10 percent contained human remains, often placed thousands of years after the structures were constructed. And what's more, a disproportionate number of dolmens are aligned to the rising of Orion on the winter solstice or spring equinox.

The dolmens throughout the western Caucasus bordering the Black Sea build on this concept. They feature a solid entrance stone with a central hole to allow telluric current to enter the monument at a prescribed time of the year. Thus the full frequency of the Sun, Moon or constellation would refill and amplify the energy already contained in the monument, least of all because dolmens sit on energy vortices. Uprights framing the entrance stone are marked with zigzag patterns indicating the flow of current, a motif common to many ancient cultures.

Since the hole is large enough to allow access for vermin, it undermines the point of protecting a body from desecration, proving such places were not designed with burial in mind. Furthermore, the culturally shared orientation associated with death is west or northwest, and very few dolmens reference this direction.

When the design reached Sardinia, the dolmen and the passage mound were fused into one, to which was added a curved frontal court resembling a crescent moon. Seen from above, the shape suggests it is attracting an invisible object toward a central collection point—in this case the hole at the bottom of a massive vertical slab beyond which lies a narrow stone passage resembling a vessel. Officially, these ubiquitous passage mounds are called *tomba di giganti*, but since the bodies of giants throughout Sardinia were uncovered in ordinary graves and never inside the mounds, it is obvious that tomb is the wrong choice of word. Given the shape described earlier, *repository* seems more appropriate.

Having visited hundreds of dolmens in a dozen countries, they never bore me, as one might suspect after so much repetition. Each one is an individual character in its own right and ought to be respected as such. On occasion, they share a common function, acting as access points for a specific entity.

In southern Britain, where I spent most of my formative years, two dolmens stand out from the rest. Standing in heather moorland on the tip of Cornwall, with a breathtaking view of the Atlantic Ocean, Chŭn Quoit was once a round barrow, now all but eroded by rain, leaving behind a delightful, mushroom domed capstone supported by four upright slabs. It comes with a folklore describing how it marks the resting place of a giant.

The other site is Spinners Rock in Devon. Like Chŭn Quoit, it is what remains of an eroded barrow. The name memorialized in folklore gives proper shape to the swirling energy still unfolding within.

Having connected with both over the course of several visits, I finally came to understand how they are still active portals used by a group entity nicknamed Shining Ones. These gods once walked in humanoid form some 10,000 years ago, before their incarnation cycle came to a close. Historically, they are connected with the Armenian Highlands, Sumeria, even Tiwanaku and the Andes, but the largest surviving documentation exists in Egypt, where they were formally known as Aku Shemsu Hor, *Shining Ones, Followers of Horus.*

We came across their handiwork earlier. They are the same gods whose deeds are described on the walls of the temple of Edfu, *the only divine beings who knew how temples and sacred sites are built.* Their understanding of the laws of nature assured the protection of portals through the temple building program they initiated up and down the Nile. Their knowledge of the laws also enabled them to transform ordinary space into sacred space. In other words, they harnessed portals already existing on the land, to which they added their own. There are natural portals and manufactured portals. The temple culture we see today in Egypt, and what it inspired beyond, is a legacy raised on the foundation of their teachings, which include many of the principles found in esoteric disciplines.

What all the locations connected with these fascinating people have in common is the sharing of sacred knowledge whose aim is the personal elevation of the individual, and collectively, the raising of global consciousness.

But Spinners Rock, Chŭn Quoit, and the Shining Ones share one further connection with Egypt. Having made dowsing maps of the energy at both sites, I later had the opportunity to do the same around the perimeter of the Great Pyramid of Giza. All three are near identical. They resemble a culturally shared form known throughout the ancient world as the symbol of balance and harmony: the *swastika*.

Many years later, the significance of these interactions took on a personal tone, as I gradually realized how my evolution in *esoterica* has been guided by these same individuals, whom I have visually encountered on several occasions and refer to them affectionately as *The Management*.

If portals are the points of reconnection with a source of knowledge, and the temples protecting them are the places of learning, the plan has proven an exceptionally good investment.

THE SCIENCE OF PORTALS

———— ꝫ┼ɛ ————

*I*n 2008, scientists at NASA astonished the world when they announced the discovery of a network of portals that opens every eight minutes above the Earth, linking this planet to the Sun and probably beyond.

In daring to employ the word *portals* in the press release, the space agency accomplished a milestone in itself.

These hitherto unknown electron diffusion regions, or *X-points*, are locations where the Earth's magnetic field connects with the Sun's to create an uninterrupted flow of particles between the two stellar bodies. Some *X-points* are small and brief, while others are vast and sustained, typically located a few thousand miles above the atmosphere, where the geomagnetic field interacts with the solar wind.

Imagine them as invisible tubes, magnetically attracting each other to generate highways in space.

All it took to find these portals was a properly equipped spacecraft. Thanks to rapid developments in technology, we finally have the tools required to render otherwise unseen phenomena, and suddenly, what once was considered science fiction, even myth, is now science *fact*.

And yet the inhabitants of southern India were already onto this concept more than 10,000 years ago. The Vedas (*knowledge*) are a vast literary work comprising four volumes and subdivisions. Brimming with allegory and metaphor, sometimes bewildering to the modern mind, the Vedas have been copied, recopied, and promulgated for thousands of years, yet their remote origin is proved by their description of *sangams* or academies where the texts were originally prepared. Since each *sangam* lasted about 4000 years before being destroyed by transgressions of the ocean, the earliest Indian *sangam* existed some 16,000 years in the past. The current or fifth *sangam* exists today in Maduray on the coast of southern India.

The importance of NASA's discovery is that it repeats, in modern language, how the authors of the *Yajurveda* described the flow of subtle energy between Earth and cosmos: *Snakes whichsoever move along the Earth, which are in sky and heaven... which are the arrows of sorcerers.*

Whenever ancient writers wished to convey a difficult concept for the average or illiterate person to grasp, they often employed metaphors, particularly the use of imagery borrowed from the observation of nature. Serpents, dragons or snakes were generally drafted into service when it was necessary to describe earth energy, because the motion of such *reptilia* visually demonstrate the twisting, flowing motion of electromagnetic current. In doing so the authors of *Yajurveda* revealed they were well aware of such telluric currents and how these are not tethered to the surface of the planet but flow toward the atmosphere and beyond. And they did so without the support of millions of dollars or hard technology by developing their inherent ability to sense the unseen, or by any number of possibilities, including an inherited science, long since forgotten.

The rest of the quote—*the arrows of sorcerers*—is also very revealing, for a *sorcerer* is a person who harnesses natural forces to connect with the source of nature. Such individuals in the Middle East were called *magi*, from whence developed the term *magician*. People who developed such latent abilities were capable of directing telluric currents for all manner of purposes: healing, personal attuning, shamanism, the levitation of megaliths, and so on. This was considered practical magic, insofar as magic is nothing more than a manipulation of the laws of nature. Nowadays, we call it *science*.

NASA has been particularly coy about admitting whether their magnetic portals connect with ancient places of veneration. It would be odd if they didn't, because even back in 1931, after exhaustive research of countless ancient sites, the French archaeologists Merle and Diot concluded that telluric currents connect all such places. Without exception.

One area they explored was the region of Brittany in northwestern France, repository of the world's greatest megalithic metropolis. In its heyday, it resembled what amounted to a vast plain of standing stones. A survey conducted at the end of the nineteenth century revealed a concentration of more than 40,000 megaliths, mounds, stone avenues, menhirs, dolmens, and other monuments. Yet the figure represented only a fraction of what remained following centuries of Church sponsored vandalism, when the systematic wrecking of monuments and stones and temples was fervently encouraged, along with the repurposing of stones for building material. Entire villages such as Crucuno and Carnac are constructed from dismembered sacred sites. Many still lie hidden in forests, even beneath the ocean from which they reappear at low tide, or on islands cut off from the mainland due to rising seas 5,000 years ago.

Around the village of Carnac, one of four surviving stone avenues alone consists of 4,000 elements arranged in thirteen parallel rows, up to a mile in length. They begin and end in egg-shaped enclosures of stone, that stand above deposits of water where the air is easily ionized. The height of the stones increases from two feet to as much as thirteen the closer they get to their respective circles.

Wandering around the region today, one gets the impression the sites were collecting something, perhaps an invisible force that was used for all manner of creative functions long since forgotten.

At least that was my first impression. Taking a casual walk in Carnac after a particularly feisty lunch of fresh seafood and snails, I was drawn into a shop by the unmistakable aroma of old paper. It was your typical bucket-and-spade store so beloved of beachgoers, yet in the rear, stacked between sandals and other odes to the plastics industry, was a thin book which, by all accounts, ought to have revolutionized the way we look at megaliths. Instead, the booklet, written by an electrical engineer by the name Pierre Mereux, hardly caused a ripple.

Pierre conducted an exhaustive study of the Carnac monuments and found that every stone serves a deliberate function in the processing of energy. His analysis reveals how dolmens amplify and release telluric energy throughout the day, with the strongest readings occurring at dawn. The voltage and magnetic variations he measured follow a scientific phenomenon known as *electric induction*: thus, a dolmen behaves like a coil or solenoid in which currents are induced and provoked by variations of the local magnetic field. And yet these phenomena are not produced with any intensity unless the stones are rich in quartz—which they are, explaining why the megaliths were quarried and transported from so far away.

The readings he took reveal an energy field that pulsates at regular intervals from around the base of the stones. These pulses are both positively and negatively charged, and when seen from above and drawn on paper, they resemble ripples in a pond, spreading out from one upright stone by as much as thirty-six feet.

I refer to this as the stone's aura, a kind of business card containing the sum of information it collects. So whereas you and I might see the physical boundary of the stone, its true size, energetically speaking, is more than four times greater in diameter.

Using his electrical apparatus, Mereux went on to find that the pulsations recycle approximately every seventy minutes, demonstrating how stones, particularly menhirs, charge and discharge on a regular basis. He also observed how the stone circles concentrate energy like a condenser, while dolmens behave like electrical coils.

But the best part of the story is, Mereux was a skeptic. He refused to believe ancient megalithic structures served any practical purpose whatsoever. As far as this French electrical engineer was concerned, it was all New Age mumbo jumbo. In the end, he proved himself wrong and validated what pagans, magi and New Agers have known all along: that megalithic monuments attract and give physical shape to an invisible force that not only flows along the Earth like serpents, but by its very nature interacts with a pulsating magnetic field out in space.

The architects of Carnac could have made life easier for themselves by erecting their monuments closer to the quarry, sixty miles away, but they didn't. Instead, they chose the location because it lies in direct relationship to hotspots of terrestrial magnetism—as do all concentrations of ancient monuments around the world. The megaliths serve to acupuncture this force, amplifying it, and in the process generate a unique interface between Earth and sky: a portal.

ADD HUMAN INTENT

In the late 1980s, Princeton Engineering Anomalies Research decided to find out if thoughts, emotions, or intent can influence the energy field around a person. After rigorous experiments using directed human thought to influence the random movement of objects, even alter the tempo of a computerized drumbeat—with verifiable results, I might add—the small team of scientists took their investigation a stage further by attempting to validate that grey area where science and mysticism meet.

This led to the creation of an electronic device called a Random Event Generator, or REG. The machine was first employed in the Global Consciousness Project, in which gathered data revealed spikes in collective human consciousness prior to major events such as a catastrophic tsunami in Indonesia. In other words, consistent deviations from expected randomicity in data were found in situations where groups became unified by something of common interest. The evidence demonstrated the existence of a field of consciousness, and intentions or emotional states that structure this field can be detected by the REG.

Encouraged, the team moved their attention to sacred sites. The scientists were intrigued as to whether the sacredness of places was due to their collective use over time, or because they were imbued with a certain energetic resonance to begin with, or because a combination of forces such as stone, electromagnetism and so forth made them so.

During an initial experiment at Mato Tipila—a Native American landscape temple in Wyoming—the REG's output was demonstrably affected by a medicine man ceremony. The team then decided to see what effect meditation groups would have on the output of the machine when chanting or meditating at interesting sites that were not necessarily sacred. The results were disappointing, influencing the machine to a small statistical degree.

Then they went to Egypt and conducted experiments at twenty-seven sites including Karnak, Luxor, and the pyramids of Giza. What astonished Princeton's team leader was that the results were higher whenever he walked around the sites in respectful silence, with a portable version of the machine in his pocket. For him, this proved that the spirit of place itself registered effects as high as the power emanating from a meditating group.

But while the temples by themselves resonated a high degree of consciousness, the combination of focused group meditation *plus* the temple created an expanded consciousness field whose effects were six times that of ordinary REG trials in the field; in fact, they represented the largest ever seen.

And there's the crux of the matter: when the human temple interacts with the stone temple, consciousness expands beyond the limits of this physical plane and stretches to another plateau—which is one of the functions of a portal.

THE BREATH OF SACRED PLACE

Another notable large-scale experiment to prove that ancient sacred sites indeed interact with telluric forces was conducted in southern Britain, at Stonehenge, and the world's largest stone circle, Avebury.

Electrodes planted in and around these henge monuments reveal how their surrounding ditches break the transmission of telluric ground current by conducting its electricity into the ditch, concentrating and releasing it at the entrance to each site at twice the rate of the surrounding land. This led to the realization that stone circles behave like concentrators of energy, just as Mereux proved earlier.

The same is true of nearby mounds such as Silbury Hill. Sil-bury— meaning *hill of the shining being*—is constructed as seven circular terraces using alternating layers of organic and inorganic material, then cloaked with a slope of chalk executed precisely at an angle of 60 degrees. Its geometry and composition allow the hill to behave like a natural battery as it soaks up the electrical current generated by the natural action of water percolating through the porous chalk soil below. The process is known as *adsorption*. To expand the effect, the hill also stands on the course of a major telluric current flowing into Avebury itself.

Silbury is unusual insofar as a second vortex of energy descends from the sky, making the summit the meeting place between mortal and Divine, as anyone who stands there knows only too well. Many are the occasions when visitors, including myself, have experienced the top half of the torso rotating clockwise and the lower half counterclockwise, as though reacting to two opposing whirlpools. The effect is both discombobulating and hilarious.

It is particularly strong around the two-third phase of a waxing moon, demonstrating how the hill stores and releases energy at regular intervals. The phenomenon is accompanied by the manifestation of a whopping ball of light that hovers above the summit for around twenty seconds, a sight referred to facetiously by local farmers as *a cosmic fart*, which I was fortunate to have observed when I lived nearby.

This is one reason why genuine crop circles began to appear around the periphery of Silbury in the early 1980s. These imprints that gently swirl the plants and bend the stems without damage appeared precisely at the perimeter of Silbury's energy field—the type that Mereux found around the stones of Carnac. The circles also manifested along the path of the telluric current flowing through the hill.

After years of extensive analysis, crop circles were found to behave exactly like ancient sacred places, with thousands of people reporting changes in consciousness identical to those in ancient places of veneration. A number of reports were filed by people who had been skeptical of the phenomenon.

My personal involvement with the phenomenon is well documented in my international bestseller, *Secrets in the Fields*, particularly my experience of being levitated and taken out-of-body to meet the entities behind the phenomenon, an experience that changed my life as well as the course of my career. To this day, that was one of my most dramatic experiences inside a portal.

To gain a better understanding of how such places work, I undertook a yearlong project to map the energy field radiating from one of the dozens of mounds in the vicinity of Silbury. Eighty percent of excavated mounds have yielded no human remains, so clearly, they were not intended as places of burial; rather, like menhirs, they give visible shape to an otherwise invisible force. Every two weeks, I visited the site, measured the edge and polarity of each ripple radiating from the mound, and plotted the results on a computer. When assembled as a timelapse sequence and seen from above, the mound appears to breathe in and out: the ripples expand and contract and alter polarity from week to week. They were influenced by the motion of the Moon, the Earth's core, and a number of factors we have yet to comprehend.

When you realize you're been interacting not with a static pile of soil but with a living energy body, you begin to treat such places with greater reverence, much as you would a person or animal. In turn, the mounds—or megaliths, for that matter—react to your energy field when you approach them, and a mere thought of appreciation can expand the site's aura. The interaction occurs in seconds and is measurable. Just like reaching out and touching a hand in a moment of solace, a sacred site shows its appreciation whenever it is acknowledged.

The breath of sacred space is indicated by a graphic symbol. At Palenque, deep in the Mexican jungle, there are specific pyramids and buildings marked with a T-shape window to identify the space as containing the Breath of God—the symbol is shorthand for *Tayi, the word of god.* The same symbol forms the doorway into the great courtyard at Chaco Canyon in New Mexico. According to academia, the space is a *kiva;* according to the wisdom-keeper whose ancestors once lived in Chaco Canyon, and thus know more about the place than anyone with a degree, it is a port for a flying disc of the gods, otherwise known as a spaceship. I'll go with the latter, particularly since all these locations are synonymous with restricted knowledge handed to humans by gods. Indeed, compared to adjacent buildings, these possess a tangible transcendental quality, as though you really are inside a hollow tube that takes you beyond the ionosphere.

STONES AS MAGNETS

A mile to the north of Silbury lies Avebury. In the late 1990s, the site and its two connecting stone avenues was covered with electrical probes in an attempt to measure how local telluric currents interact with four-and-a-half thousand-year-old sacred site.

Surges in geomagnetic energy were detected in the stones of the two avenues, suggesting that, in their complete form, these winding causeways were placed on or aligned with areas rich in telluric current which the stones help conduct into the center of the site—much in the same way as they do in Carnac. Inside Avebury, magnetic readings at night drop to a far greater level than can be accounted for under natural circumstances. At sunrise, they charge back, with the telluric current from the surrounding land attracted to the henge, just as magnetic fluctuations at the site reach their maximum. This reveals why temple builders from England to Egypt regarded such places as living organisms that sleep at night and awake at dawn.

The way in which the megaliths are placed amplifies the effect. One ingredient for which the stones of temples were painstakingly sourced is magnetite. They are packed with it. One scientist involved with the Avebury project measured the current of its surviving sixty-seven stones and discovered that the magnetic south pole of each stone faces the next in line as you walk toward the circle. This arrangement means that the north poles of the stones oppose the local geomagnetic field, creating a defined pathway for the energy.

Inside Avebury's two small circles, the south poles of all stones point toward the following stone, in a clockwise direction, with two exceptions: the entrance megaliths have their magnetic poles aligned ninety degrees to their companions. In turn, these align with the stones of the avenue leading *into* the circle rather than with those of the circle itself.

In essence, Avebury is a series of deliberately aligned magnets. Its architects were following the same principle behind a modern atomic particle collider, in which airborne ions are steered in one direction.

INTERACTING WITH ENERGY

Similar effects have been detected at sites throughout Britain. The average intensity of the geomagnetic field inside stone circles is significantly lower than outside, as though the stones act as a force field. Where the monument is in relatively good shape—such as Swinside, Callanish and Brodgar—it is possible at certain times of the day to sense this protective zone as it interacts with the nodes on the palms of an outstretched hand, where some of the body's most sensitive electrical points are found. The effect generates a tingling sensation on the skin.

Then there's the association between the placing of standing stones relative to fault lines, as is the case with the Scottish stone circles. In Brittany, the densest distribution of standing stones coincides with France's most active geological faults. In essence, the quartz rich stones are in a permanent state of subtle vibration that, in turn, generates a piezoelectric effect.

Archaeologists working in Scotland often report tubes of light and other luminous phenomena interacting with the stones; or how the megaliths emit an ultrasonic hum that is captured on sensitive equipment just before sunrise, the time when the earth's electromagnetic field is at its most potent. Needles on electrical equipment are known to go off the scale when crossing the perimeter of stone circles at this time of day, while some equipment stops functioning altogether. It brings to mind a discipline used in ancient Egyptian temples—and elsewhere I imagine—whereby the initiate was moved from temple to temple to slowly raise the body's electrical current so as not to overload its circuits, in preparation for entering that large cosmic battery, the Great Pyramid, a process that took anywhere between three to ten years of preparation.

The pre-dawn effect may just turn out to be the most important discovery at megalithic sites because it is the time when an exterior force interacts with the local electromagnetic environment to generate a link between temple and sky. It works like this: every morning, the Earth is subjected to a rise in the solar wind, which intensifies the planet's geomagnetic field. At night, this field weakens, then picks up at dawn and the cycle repeats. At this point the geomagnetic field interacts with telluric currents flowing along the surface of the Earth, intensifying the current, which in turn is drawn to nearby sacred sites.

These invisible rivers travel better along soil with a high content of metal and water, and probably quartz. Where a boundary between two different types of geology occurs, a telluric current crossing either reinforces or weakens the daily fluctuations of the local geomagnetic field. This generates a hotspot of energy called a *conductivity discontinuity*, and even though ancient people did not own state of the art diagnostic equipment, they were capable of locating such portals long before scientists built machines to prove them right. The Lakota of North America refer to this interaction with a far more memorable name: *skan*.

They claim that when *skan* concentrates at power places, it influences the mind and elevates personal power in the form of spiritual attuning. In essence, the energy raises the human body's resonance. So, when one visits and interacts with multiple power places, the energy builds inside the body. It is this quality that leads to a numinous state of mind. You begin to feel a transcendence, you start to perceive other levels of reality, and, under the right conditions, in a very tangible manner. It is no coincidence, then, that large concentrations of petroglyphs happen to coincide with these *conductivity discontinuities*. Such clusters of energy were sensed and then guided to assist the shamanic state, and what was observed in the Otherworld was remembered and carved in symbolic form upon the rocks, be it a cosmic truth, a revelation, or a facet of the mechanics of nature.

Such panels dot the desert landscapes of Utah and Arizona, often in hard-to-reach locations, ensuring their survival while simultaneously offering a dome of stillness in which the serious inquirer can pause and reflect.

I remember one such occasion while attending a conference in one of the most disturbed environments I've ever encountered: a casino in Laughlin, Nevada. No, it was worse, it was hell. After two days inside an environment where the skin appeared to turn pallid, I began bribing people to drive me away, beyond the city limits and into the wilderness and shoot me, so toxic was this building in the middle of nowhere. I knew nothing of the area. I just needed to wash my body and mind of an impurity that clung to me like alien ectoplasm.

We drove off road and into the desert a few miles beyond the city. Hilly territory. Making straight for a sandstone cliff that seemed to be beckoning me, I had not expected to come face-to-face with an entire rock face covered with hundreds of petroglyphs. It looked like a Native American newspaper. I vividly recall the moment I approached this wall of symbols and feeling every drop of negative energy melt away. In minutes, I was transformed, restored, the life force within returning to balance along with color to my skin. So entrancing was this portal that I even walked without fear past the only critters of which I have a phobia.

Snakes.

INFLUENCING THE MIND

The interaction between astral and terrestrial energies alone does not make a portal a sacred place. A portal becomes sacred when it energizes within us feelings and concepts we associate with the spiritual dimensions of life. This perceptual reality, experienced and reinforced over long spans of time, is what marks sacred space from an otherwise regular part of the landscape.

The process of transformation within the individual is due, in part, to the effect telluric forces exert on the pineal gland, particularly when they are concentrated. Fluctuations in the geomagnetic field affect the production of chemicals made by the pineal, such as *pinoline*, which interacts with another neurochemical in the brain, *serotonin*, the end product being the creation of DMT, a hallucinogen that allows information to be more readily received. In an environment where geomagnetic field intensity is decreased, people are known to experience psychic and shamanic states.

A second process involves magnetism. Blood flowing through the veins carries a fair amount of dissolved iron, so when one enters a concentrated magnetic environment, this force interacts with the iron in the bloodstream, much like a magnet reorganizes iron filings on a sheet on paper.

The same is true of the brain. Substantial amounts of magnetite are found in brain tissue and the cerebral cortex. Under the right conditions, magnetic stimulation induces dreamlike states, even in waking consciousness, something to consider next time you walk around a megalithic site with all those stones brimming with magnetite.

The human body is now widely accepted to be a walking electromagnetic edifice, sensitive to minute fluctuations, particularly DNA, which receives information from changes in the local electromagnetic environment. With telluric forces playing such a pivotal role in the function of portals, their influence on the body, especially bone, with all its silica through which electrical signals flow, is obvious.

In essence, it can be argued that a portal is made of the very stuff that makes us who we are. It is a mirror of the human body and the instrument with which it peers into the Otherworld.

OF REBIRTH, DRAGONS, AND GREEN MEN

———— ⋹†⋸ ————

eligion comes from the Latin *religio*. It means *to reconnect*.

Reconnecting with the source of things is an admirable aim in life. It is the bedrock of the seeker, least of all because one no longer feels lost and alone from the moment they wake up in the morning. Reconnecting has served as the foundation of every spiritual culture on the planet and remains the core belief in esoteric tradition to this day.

The chief method of reconnecting to the source was through initiation, and the instructions were to be found in *The Way of the Gods* and other sacred teachings, which came under the umbrella term *Mysteries*.

Indian sages still make the distinction among members of the public who have been initiated into the Mysteries and those who have not. They refer to the former as the *living*; by contrast, the uninitiated are born, endure a difficult life, and arrive unfulfilled at death. They are the *corpses*.

When the *Mysteries* teachings reached the Greek world, the benefits were promoted by philosophers such as Plato: *Those who are initiated into the great mysteries perceive a wondrous light. Purer regions are reached, and fields where there is singing and dancing, sacred words and divine visions, inspire a holy awe. Then the man, perfected and initiated, free and able to move super-*

physically, without constraint, celebrates the mysterious with a crown on his head. He lives among pure men and saints. He sees on earth the many who have not been initiated and purified, buried in the darkness, and through fear of death, clinging to their ills for want of belief in the happiness of the beyond.

Plato pointed out that the aim of the philosopher—or anyone, for that matter—is to become conscious of the wisdom found only in the super-physical reality of the Otherworld while still living: *True philosophers make dying their profession, and to them of all people death is least alarming...[for they are] glad to set out for the place where there is the prospect of attaining the object of their lifelong desire, which is Wisdom.... If one is a real philosopher, one will be of the firm belief that one will never find Wisdom in all its purity in any other place.*

Only a fool would resist this opportunity to experience the root of reality and return fully enlightened. Who wouldn't wish to walk through life in charge of the helm of their destiny? The experience of two worlds makes you present in both but bound to neither.

As the Mysteries spread through the Near East, they inspired the foundation of sects such as the Mandeans and Essenes, who promoted a *living resurrection* to anyone who was curious enough to experience it. It was such an empowering tool that it became the central credo of emerging gnostic Christianity, as the apostle Philip himself stated: *Those who say they will die first and then rise are in error. If they do not first receive the resurrection while they live, when they die, they will receive nothing.*

In other words, those who believe in a literal interpretation of resurrection are confusing a spiritual truth with an actual event.

But the common point in this thread is that all this metaphoric dying to access the Otherworld was taking place in energetically sensitive locations, be they sacred caves, holy mountains, or ancient temples—the portals where the laws of nature facilitate the process.

THINGS TAKE A LEFT TURN

As *religio* corrupted into the blind dogma of organized religion—as it did in Europe by 400 A.D.—the portals and the ancient structures that protected them became an impediment to recruiting the masses. Peasants may have been largely illiterate back then, but they did understand what worked and what didn't. They knew from direct experience how places of veneration contributed to the wellbeing of the land and the individual, they sensed how certain hotspots promoted healing, even facilitated fertility in barren women.

When you have access to such free physical and spiritual healthcare, you are not want to give up on a tradition. Consequently, attendance of stone circles, menhirs and dolmens was outlawed, the veneration of sacred wells and trees and caves forbidden. Penalties for non-compliance ranged from fasting for three years to death.

When this policy failed to motivate the public, churches were built over the old pagan places, obliterating all traces of the former structures or incorporating them into the fabric of the new buildings. And yet the builders failed to grasp that the monuments they were supplanting were not necessarily the main attractor. They were marking, storing, and protecting an invisible portal.

Ironically, the focal point of a new church was sited over the highest concentration of telluric current. There's a reason why it's called the *altar*. In Old English, *altar* was spelled *alter*, and together with its Latin root, *alterare*, it identifies the location as both a place of altering and a portal for elevating. It took generations for the authorities to cotton on to this by limiting access to the altar to all except the priest or bishop. To this day, a sign warning parishioners *Do Not Pass Into This Sacred Space* hangs from a thick red rope barring the curious from the altar of the main cathedral of Wellington, New Zealand.

You might think that thousands of years of tradition of accessing portals had finally ended, but you'd be wrong. There were people embedded within the system who understood the ancient ways and felt compelled to preserve them, stone masons being the chief conspirators. As we saw earlier, a portal is either the result of a singular vortex springing from the Earth, or the culmination of converging forces fed by telluric currents. As such, there are many places one can sit inside a church or Gothic cathedral and still connect with the source.

You just need to know what symbols to look for.

THERE BE SERPENTS AND DRAGONS

The sensible way to reach Mont St. Michel is by shuttle bus, but for those with a death wish, the proper route is on foot over quicksand. They say the closer you are to danger, the further you are from harm. As far as this portal goes, I've been far from harm three times. If it was good enough for thousands of years for pilgrims, it's good enough for me. Of course, many didn't make it all the way across the treacherous bay, the route is also a sandy graveyard, but we'll skip that part.

On a calm and sunny day, there is the bonus during the three hour hike of an uninterrupted view of the sinuous tidal flats, the shimmering island Tombelaine—repository of the Gaulish Sun god Bel—and beyond it the blue grey of the cantankerous English Channel. And the best view of Mont St. Michel itself, a steep lump of rock resilient in the face of fierce tides that rush through every day resembling a wall of charging stallions. The pilgrim path is the longest route to reach the holy island, but it partly follows two of the Earth's most studied telluric currents, dubbed Apollo and Athena by the dowser Hamish Miller.

Long before the impressive cathedral was built, Mont St. Michel was a place of spiritual significance with roots lost in prehistory. The remains of a giant's grave on the summit conveniently marks the *node,* the spot where the two currents intertwine. Changes in culture led to the site falling into disuse until one night in 706 A.D. when Aubert, Bishop of Avranches, received a visit from Archangel Michael with a request to erect a chapel on the island to rekindle interest in this forgotten portal. Given the difficulty of building a structure on such a remote location, Aubert shrugged and went back to sleep. Being the persistent type, Michael returned and burned a hole in his head. That did the trick, and soon after, Aubert's chapel was erected at the base of the island, conveniently in-between the two telluric currents.

Apollo and Athena weave their way up and around the mount until they converge inside the cathedral, where you'd lose track of them had crafty stonemasons not left clues of their whereabouts. The attentive pilgrim will pace the cloister and notice how certain pillars feature the carving of a dragon or serpent. The same motifs repeat throughout the nave, skulking in corners or peering from the capitals of stone columns. Follow these creatures and you will be led to a subterranean room with two ancient altars nestled side by side in a chamber refurbished from an early Roman chapel, which itself was built from the stones of the dilapidated Neolithic passage mound.

It seems everyone has been marking this portal. It is very rare for two altars to occupy a sanctuary, but here, deep inside the bowels of the cathedral, they each mark the path of Apollo and Athena where they intertwine like two mating serpents. The eddies from this friction of energy are felt in the room above, the exact spot marked by a set of curved tiles inset into the granite floor and placed at an awkward angle relative to the otherwise balanced geometry of the room.

As we have already seen, telluric currents wander and wave unless anchored by stones purposefully selected for the purpose. This action was personified in the symbol of a serpent pinned down by a rod held by an *augur,* a member of an elite priesthood responsible for locating the sacred center of cities, choosing the site of temples and assessing their preferred time of construction. In the Greco-Roman era, these adepts belonged to the College of Augurs, along with their counterparts, the *Oiônistai*. Their work—and name—is still commemorated in the noun describing the opening of an important place or event: *in-augur-ation*.

An early image of an *augur* piercing a serpent can be found carved on a wall in the temple of Edfu, but if you happen to be in the cathedral city of Wells, England, you can see them on either side of a limestone staircase, as though marking the passage of an unseen force. Dressed in a monk's habit, each figure holds a stick that is deftly inserted into the mouth of each serpent, upon whose coiled bodies the figures stand. And indeed, a feminine telluric current does flow up the gently curving staircase and into a magnificent octagonal chapel.

Bathed in natural light, the chapel is raised by thirty-two vaults supported by a central column resembling a palm tree, making it the thirty-third—as in *degrees of Freemasonry*.

Officially, the room served as a meeting place for the conduct of civic affairs, yet it is impossible to conduct a conversation with a person five feet away. I shared this observation with an astute tour guide whose followers were having a hard time hearing her. *I agree*, she confided in me, *the geometry of the room is designed to break up words*. It does, however, possess the best acoustics I've ever heard, ideal for the movement of sound, particularly toning, and many have been the hours spent here humming a note with fellow pilgrims and becoming entranced.

The chapter house in Wells Cathedral fuses geometry, masonry, light, sound, telluric current, and potentized water beneath the building to generate a portal of unparalleled grace. It serves as a rare example in any event, even more so in the charged political and religious climate of thirteenth century Europe.

TO KILL OR NOT TO KILL THE DRAGON

In time, the symbol of the anchored serpent was turned into propaganda, with saints George and Michael shown killing the dragon outright. It was a deft use of marketing with the intention of signaling to people of the Middle Ages the death of old traditions. And in case they didn't buy the message, the serpent was further downgraded as the logo of all evil.

By contrast, dragons in the Far East were not slain; rather, their electrical power was harnessed and channeled to many aspects of daily life. The proper flow of energy is central to *Feng Shui*, and to ensure a favorable outcome, entire hillsides were reshaped to prevent obstacles impeding the dragon. It was believed that correct flow of energy and the portals with which it is connected assured the vitality of the individual and society as a whole. Only an unstable dragon was considered dangerous and required subduing by grounding, traditionally using metal rods planted into the soil. This is one reason why the dragon became the symbol of temporal power assigned to a magician or sorcerer, who in turn took on the title *Son of Heaven*.

Images of this earth acupuncture are found throughout sacred art, just as they are on megaliths. Careful observation of menhirs in Brittany and Portugal reveals a series of carved serpents issuing from the base of these phallic stones to indicate the precise position where energy has been anchored. But as the old tradition gradually declined due to a shift to urban society, the intellectualizing of the old ways saw many serpent stones fall by the wayside, some incorporated into walls of cathedrals, others pulled down and carved into gate posts for farmyards or broken up for roads and railways. Those that survive retain their power, courtesy of an army of devotees who restore their energy through ritual, particularly at sacred times such as the solstice and equinox.

In rural parts of France it was still an accepted practice in the last century for barren women to approach a menhir and rub it between their thighs to induce fertility. One picture postcard from Britanny shows maidens dancing around such a monolith on the fertility feast of Beltane to honor and revitalize the spirit held within the stone.

One of the most dramatic demonstrations of the power held by these portal stones presented itself during a tour of megaliths in Brittany. On the outskirts of the village of Dol there stands what several members of the group remarked as *a really big stone*. At thirty-one feet above the soil, the Menhir de Champ-Dolent is impressive, I agree, but it's just a warmup for the two over in Finnistere.

The menhir felt particularly vibrant, so I decided to conduct a demonstration. I dowsed the ripples of energy generated by the monolith, then inserted one of my copper rods into the soil to mark the edge of its surrounding field—the stone's *soul*, as it were. I was about to return to the stone when *The Management* compelled me to return, walk twice as far from the rod, and trace a marker on the soil just behind a picnic bench placed in the field by the tourism board. *What good is a picnic without a watching menhir*, I wondered sarcastically. I had a strange premonition about this unusual request when one of the men asked if he could sit out the ceremony. He'd joined the tour to keep his partner company but was a wee bit skeptical of what we were up to. And that's fine by me. One should never force this stuff onto others, they join of their own volition.

He sat on the picnic table to watch sixteen people join hands and just about cover the girth of this stone giant. Yes, it was *that* big. We tuned into the stone, toned, and felt the stone vibrate. The more we toned, the stronger the effect. It became hard to disentangle. A few minutes into the ritual I heard a dull thud from behind, and I remember thinking, *Hmm, that's going to hurt*.

We finally stopped. Exhausted but tingling.

Curious as to whether the toning had any effect on the energy field of the stone, I took the remaining rod and measured the ripples. Not only had they increased in number, they now extended well beyond the original perimeter.

We'd managed to double the diameter of the stone's soul. Meanwhile, the gentleman who'd sat on the picnic table raised himself off the ground, dazed and dusty. As he describes it, there was a moment during our toning when an invisible force knocked him down. I looked at the spot where he fell and there was the mark I'd made earlier. It was now the edge of the expanded energy field.

He'd literally been bowled over by a wall of energy.

SERPENTS ON THE LAND

Sometimes the serpent symbol hides in plain sight. The highest concentrated energy in Avebury stone circle is in a section called The Cove, still marked by two of three original monoliths; together they once formed a receptacle, a cup. Should your sensing faculties be switched off, you are reminded of this portal when the midday sun casts its light upon the lozenge stone to bring out the carved relief of a curving serpent, the head still recognizable after 4,500 years of weathering.

Just like the aforementioned Apollo and Athena, two other well-studied telluric currents overlap inside The Cove. Flowing down the spine of southern England, the Michael and Mary currents are named for the preponderance of chapels and churches placed on their respective paths and dedicated to these Christian figures, along with holy wells, menhirs, Gothic cathedrals, dolmens, and tree circles—over 800 in all, with Avebury placed roughly at the center.

It is a sight best appreciated by a high flying bird, as is Avebury itself. The massive stone circle and its two leading avenues resemble a five mile long, pregnant serpent.

Follow Mary's serpentine flow and it will guide you twenty miles northeast to the chalk escarpment of Uffington, a place synonymous with earth energy and ritual. Its richness of fecundity has lured pilgrims here since the Neolithic era, so much so that the trail became Britain's oldest public footpath, the Ridgeway. Still accessible to everyone, many fresh air lovers undertake the weeklong walk among some of England's most bucolic scenery.

Hiking towards the summit of Uffington brings you to a conical, truncated mound, shaped from the chalk. Legend states that Dragon Hill was named when St. George saw a dragon there and skewered the hapless creature on the spot, and to this day, the spilled blood has left a white patch where no grass grows, no matter how many times it is reseeded.

This is clearly a Christianized reworking of a longstanding pagan tradition because the Mary current does indeed flow up from the valley, forms a spiral around the mound, and dips into the bald chalk patch. Compasses sometimes behave erratically above the spot, as do people who happen to stand there when the energy is recharging, particularly at dawn on the winter solstice, when the first shaft of sunlight selectively lights up Dragon Hill prior to the surrounding landmarks.

Uffington is a deliberately designed ritual landscape utilizing the power of the reborn Sun to charge a portal given visible shape as a white mound, illustrating the cleverness of our ancestors to bind the power of the land to the Sun in a dramatic, almost theatrical style.

A CHEROKEE SERPENT

England's landscape serpents have a cousin in North America, the aptly named Serpent Mound of Ohio. The coiled earthwork resembling a serpent eating an egg is still in remarkably good shape despite it having been created before the Cherokee arrived after trekking across the central plains. And that was many thousands of years ago. In their tradition, the Cherokee inherited the mound from the Alewani, a tribe of giant people who were its true builders. The newly arrived Cherokee found what little remained of the tribe and took up stewardship of the site.

Why the Alewani chose this hilltop over the myriad of locations in the region remained a mystery until late twentieth century technology revealed the site to mark the edge of an impact crater from a meteorite. This *cryptoexplosive structure*, as science refers to it, was created 280 million years ago, long enough for all trace of its cosmic origin to be obliterated, and yet the Alewani must have perceived the landscape as special and different. And they were right. Magnetic and gravitational fluctuations around the eroded crater generate a fourteen mile wide portal still capable of interfering with compasses, let alone the human body and all the dissolved magnetite it contains.

My first trip to Serpent Mound was during a lull at a large conference where I was making a keynote presentation. A small and dedicated group of local researchers were keen to take me there, and I was keen to finally see this wonder. One of the gentlemen in the group, Ross Hamilton, had just written a paper outlining a hypothesis that each of the serpent's coils marked the extreme positions of the Sun and Moon. Serpent Mound is a marvelous—and accurate—astronomical marker, an idea first proposed in 1890 when it was believed the axis of the serpent's egg was oriented to the summer solstice sunset.

Still, why design it in the shape of a serpent? Perhaps it gave visual context to a tradition among the Sioux, who regard the association between a toothed serpent and the solstice as a passage marker into the Otherworld. Little else was known, and that was the sum of knowledge I took with me. As experience has shown, the less you know, the more you learn.

Treading lightly around each coil, I was surprised to feel little in terms of telluric current, demonstrating how it pays not to take sacred places for granted, they will confound your logic and surprise you. Since everything seemed to be moving toward the egg, I tagged along. As I stepped into the oval area, an electric coil seemed to rise out of the ground and shoot through my spine, and for several seconds, I was transfixed. *So this is where the energy is.* The serpent shape guides you to the point of contact.

The effect was immediate. I was shown a series of sacred sites arranged like a wheel with Serpent Mound as the hub. The images dissolved, replaced by a vision of a tunnel running under the egg and toward a cave that served a ritual function, making the cave the portal itself.

I shared this vision with those gathered. *How do you know all this, you've not been here before?* Indeed there was an entrance into a partly collapsed tunnel at the bottom of the bluff and it led toward the egg. One of the sites I described, in intricate detail, had only just been confirmed by archaeologists. It was still covered by undergrowth and trees. Nothing had been published on the matter, I couldn't have known about it.

DISSOLVING REALITY

Interacting with serpent energy takes on greater significance when experienced by the non-believer. Take the island of Iona, for instance, a rock one mile by four off the west coast of Scotland, yet it boasts one of the highest concentrations of royal burials per square foot—sixty, to be exact. Clearly the location holds some special significance for kings and queens (even one British Prime Minister) to have demanded their bodies be sent here from as far away as Denmark.

The heavy hand of St. Columba and his acolytes robbed the island of many symbols marking the repositories of earth energy. All that remains are traces of a dragon and two green men now barely discernable on the stonework in the abbey. While in the nearby Nunnery, a weather-beaten *sheela-na-gig*—an ancient fertility figure depicting a wide-eyed female with an exaggerated vulva parted wide open—gawps from a ruined stone window. Inclement weather purged the rest, and yet none of these calamities wiped the memory of Iona as a place of power. Three portals remain active, and none, as one might assume, in the celebrated abbey itself, but in the unassuming chapel beside it. To understand this, we need to roll back the clock 2,000 years.

Following threats to their lives, the Essenes fled Galilee and arrived three years later in Iona as the Culdee, a corruption of the Armenian name of the supreme god, *khaldi*. These white robed strangers were literally followers of the supreme creative force. They also believed in experiencing living resurrection, and sourced those unique points on the land where an enhanced electromagnetic signature facilitates the process. Once on Iona they erected a beehive stone chamber on a forlorn corner of the island for any monk wishing to engage with a portal in complete solitude.

The other spot is marked by said chapel. Hardly anyone pays it the attention it deserves, because the abbey next door looks better on social media, especially if you're in the foreground of the photo. But to those whose antenna is tuned to the right frequency, it's a place of blissful immersion. That the Culdee performed the living resurrection ritual here is commemorated in a local legend, in which the walls of the chapel came down as fast as they went up, as though by evil intent, and only when a person was buried alive would the stones remain upright.

A few centuries of dilapidation left the chapel in ruin, until Columba and his right-hand man, Odhràn, arrived in the sixth century and undertook a renovation of the buildings on Iona. To Odhràn, the legend sounded like hogwash, the work of the devil, so to prove the old superstitions wrong he volunteered for the task of being buried alive. When the soil was removed three days later, the flabbergasted monk raised himself out of the hole and declared *all that has been said of hell is a joke*. It appears that during his interment in this portal, he experienced something beyond the ordinary living state. Just as Plato once suggested, he was shown the true nature of reality.

If only Odhràn had interpreted the legend as allegory: the falling and raising of walls refers to the parting of the veil between physical and non-physical realities.

GREETING THE GREEN MAN

Perhaps it became politically incorrect for stonemasons to carve serpents all over the alleged houses of God, especially after the slithery things acquired the burden of evil, so they resorted to another symbol to help the heathen readily identify pockets of energy in sacred places.

There are more effigies of the green man in northern European churches than images of Jesus and Mary; Wells Cathedral alone boasts no less than twenty-two. How did they get away with such a patently pagan image? Perhaps bishops saw the image of a strange man with vegetation emerging from its mouth as benign, an artistic whimsy, and allowed it to procreate at will from door to pillar. Yet like the serpent and dragon, the green man is another potent symbol of the life force.

Sometimes the green man is the greeter, his foliated face beaming approvingly by the entrance to an old church. The effigy marks the door through which telluric current flows, beyond whose threshold one is entranced. To further remind that you are entering into a communion with a space dedicated to the fertility of body and mind, the receding arches framing the doorway portray the labial ridges of female genitalia. One is literally entering the womb of a Divine woman, the queen of heaven, goddess of the Otherworld, thence to be transported down the nave (from *navis*, a boat), and disembarking where these forces converge at the portal, the altar.

Such is the hidden language of sacred buildings.

Our ancestors were under no illusion that nature is a recurring phenomenon, a never ending drama between life, death, and rebirth. Just as all signs of the life force seem depleted by December 20th, so its triumphant resurgence begins the following day. Nature is a dying, rejuvenating god, the green man its poster boy. It may seem odd to ascribe the position to a male figure without realizing that nature is represented by a Divine bride. At the lowest ebb of the year, the green man descends into the Otherworld for three days to consummate the Divine marriage, and in doing so he returns resurrected, verdant, and virile for another year. Just like nature. As such, the green man mythos is the European variation of the passion play between Isis and Osiris, whose alchemical wedding resurrected Osiris as Horus, on December 25th no less.

Among the last practitioners of the natural and magical arts during the Middle Ages, the Knights Templar and their sister organization, the Order of Cister, are probably the best known. Their prime monuments are found in the town of Tomar, Portugal. One church is dedicated to their hero, John the Baptist, and it is packed with green men, so many that I use it as a test of observation for *info-dels* who attend my tours.

The church has been rebuilt on top of what may have been a site of ancient veneration, and deviations from official ecclesiastic design seem to confirm this. For example, the altar is not placed over the original energy hotspot; instead, it serves as a geodetic marker linking the Templar's most sacred monument—a sixteen-sided rotunda—to their original domicile in Jerusalem, an extraordinary feat of geomancy, given how the three sites connect across 2,000 miles.

On close inspection, one specific column in the church is singled out by no less than two green men *and* a dragon. They preside over an elegant pulpit resembling a spiral emerging from the ground. And there's the rub: whoever ascends the pulpit is entranced by the telluric current spiraling from below, probably the site of the original portal.

The Templars were great believers in fairness, and contrary to official commentators, most of them were married, with women holding equal status. To emphasize the point, a small chapel in Tomar dedicated to their patron Erea, a renaissance woman in her own right, contains a rare effigy of a green woman, the only example I've ever come across on my extensive travels.

As the persecution of the Templars by the Church reached a boiling point, they printed new business cards, changed their name to Scottish Rite Freemasons and bought themselves time to continue protecting the ancient places of veneration. At the close of the nineteenth century, a wealthy Portuguese Mason by the name Carvalho Monteiro bought an estate nestled in the bucolic mountain of Sintra, where Templars and Freemasons had practiced the sacred arts for 800 years.

The estate, Quinta da Regaleira, contains a scenographic garden designed to educate the general public about the Mysteries. And while Sintra is a gravitational anomaly in itself, the Regaleira estate is particularly endowed with hotspots of energy, so it is probably not by accident that the lane beside the estate is an ancient sacred way, while the land it occupies was once called the Forest of Angels.

One hotspot lies under an outstanding white chapel. The exterior is dressed in imagery that the average bishop would find comfortable, giving the outward impression of *nothing unusual to see here*. Closer observation reveals symbols associated with the raising of consciousness such as the pinecone, while at the rear of the building lies a green man, his mouth gaping wide, filled with rejuvenating power.

BEYOND DRAGONS AND GREEN MEN

The dragon and the green man are but two markers identifying the flow of life force in a world of censorship. Given the intrinsic relationship between portals and the spiritual rebirth of the human spirit, the promulgators of these useful markers placed their lives on the line so the of the rest of the world could maintain the connection with the miraculous.

Where these symbols are culturally redundant, they are supplemented by the trident, be it the one held by Shiva or Poseidon, so when you see it in Utah, it comes as a pleasant surprise.

Monument Valley is a wonder of nature and energy tumbling together to create one of the most hypnotic sandstone landscapes on Earth. It also has come to typify the modern world, half spiritual, half tourist hell. To avoid the latter, I work with a Navajo guide named Leroy.

I love to work with this elder because he deduced in a few minutes that our group was interested in matters of greater weight than tourism. He switched off the meter and took us to places where few white people seldom go. The first port of call was the Navajo altar, the place of baptism, where a crystal clear stream of water emerges from an otherwise barren desert to nourish a massive juniper tree hidden between two sand dunes.

Then he drove us deeper into the valley to experience the local portal. In hindsight, I believe he was testing our abilities. The site is an imposing sandstone butte into which runs a small cave. But I felt the cave to be a distraction from something of far greater importance, so instead I turned right and walked toward the vertical cliff face. There was no distinguishing mark, nothing of photogenic value, yet I was compelled to stand at this spot, and for ten minutes it felt like peace on Earth.

A-ha, said Leroy, beckoning me closer to the wall. Subtle as a puff of steam, a mark no longer than three inches etched into the red sandstone revealed the orange layer beneath in the shape of a trident. The only other occasion where I'd come across it was, ironically, a passage mound in France, also used as a place for journeying.

It seems the ancient art of sensing is still alive and well after all. Who needs dragons and green men.

FAERIES, GOBLINS, AND OTHER ALIENS
⸻ 3†Ɛ ⸻

*T*hroughout Ireland, portals come with a rich history of faeries. Protective faeries, jealous faeries, helpful faeries, vengeful faeries. They manifest in all manner of forms, as a visit to the Uragh stones will reveal.

The drive up the Rossard hills on the Beara Peninsula is delightful if you don't mind your vehicle aging a year or two. Beyond a meadow, Uragh stands meekly beside a loch with a curving mountainside and waterfall for a backdrop.

Beside its tallest monolith there often appears a woman wrapped in an aura of pearl light. She's about eight feet tall, slender, and dressed in what looks like a long satin gown. That was my first impression of her as I neared the site. I had no idea of the history behind this stone circle, but the region is known to have been settled by the Tuatha de Danaan, a magical race of half-human, half-divine people who originally migrated from the regions around the Black Sea where, as the Tuadhe d'Anu, they once held noble status. Prior to that they were the pre-diluvian gods of the Armenian highlands whose nickname was Shining Ones. These people were unusually tall with fair hair and blue eyes and compared to the indigenous people of Ireland they were described as *fair folk*—partly in acknowledgement of their light skin pigment and partly because of their demeanor, but above all, the Tuatha de Danaan possessed an unusual ability to understand the laws of nature and how to manipulate them, in the positive connotation of the word.

In time, the *fair folk* would be supplanted by other races, but their accomplishments and spirituality made them so beloved of the Irish that when the Catholic Church reached Ireland, the locals gave lip service to the newcomers while continuing private veneration of the *fair folk*. Unable to win the battle for the spirit of the land, the Church banished the Tuatha De Danaan (quite how one banishes people who've been long dead is another matter) and cast the Divine race as bloodthirsty faeries who'd suck your blood at night and lead you to the path of the devil.

And thus, the *faery* was born of the *fair folk*.

The apparition of the fair lady of Uragh may well be the residual presence of one of the Tuatha de Danaan recorded forever in the magnetic field of the stones. Unlike a ghost whose presence haunts a site due to unresolved trauma, this lady seems to have stayed on to protect the site, she is the resident spirit of place.

My unexpected encounter was later validated, without prompting, by a good friend who not only happens to be a natural and gifted medium, on occasion she also assists the police with serious cases. "Did you encounter the tall woman in white at Uragh?" asked Isabelle, casually.

The faery association with portals is particularly strong in northwestern France, whose monuments were largely erected by the same race a couple of thousand years before and thus precede those of Britain and Ireland. The aptly named Roche aux Fées (*Rock of the Faeries*) is a well-preserved passage mound, albeit minus its earthen blanket. Not only is it the largest in France, one of its megalithic architraves is as large as Stonehenge's. As usual, the mineral composition of the stones elicits a state of awareness and explains why 500 tons of them were dragged for three miles, in preference over easily obtainable local stone. Such a herculean feat is said to be the labor of faeries who erected it in a single night by dropping stones from their aprons. Faeries certainly were fast workers, because the same story of speedy construction of megalithic monuments using magic is told in Yucatan, just as they are in Tiwanaku.

Faeries are but one image presented to us mortals whenever we interact with portals, they use the same entrance to come into our reality just as we do to access theirs. There are countless varieties of entities, and they take on innumerable forms. In the spirit world (also known as *the room next door*) beings do not possess a physical body in the way we might comprehend, although they are very much physical in their level of reality. Rarely can their appearance be understood because we have no reference point, no experience from which our brain can draw. If an entity were to manifest in front of you as they appear, you'd probably be paralyzed with fear. Or wonder. Or you might do the natural thing when faced with the unfamiliar: run. To ease discomfort, entities take on a form acceptable to local regions and customs. By adapting, the interactions become less threatening. What might look like a *goblin* in northern Europe will appear in the Middle East in the form of a *djinn,* because each form conforms to a culturally shared perception of the supernatural.

When I was learning my craft, Isabelle the Medium took me and other neophytes to places of power throughout Ireland to learn to distinguish between various forms of energy, the aim being to develop our own intuitive abilities, our *inner tuition*, as I call it.

One portal we visited had been a stone circle or passage mound—the provenance is unclear—repurposed by the new religion as a cemetery. Perhaps whoever was in charge recognized the latent energy of place as beneficial to assisting souls escape the tug of gravity on their journey towards the afterlife.

Standing as a ring and holding hands, we tuned in to the energy of place, connected with the spirit of the land, asked permission to make inquiries and declared our intent to stand in hallowed ground. About thirty minutes later, we returned to normal consciousness and let our arms rest by our sides. Although I was back on *terra firma,* part of my consciousness was still enjoying the energy of the Otherworld, and for a few minutes I inhabited two levels of reality. Then came a weight on the tips of the fingers of my left hand. Someone or some *thing* was holding on to them: the height of an infant, naked, with a head resembling a beetroot mounted on a thin body with a protruding belly and spindly legs and arms like cocktail sticks.

"What the hell *are* you?" I said, raising my arm and dragging the curious creature up with it, at which point it shouted gobbledygook at me and requested, in no uncertain terms, to be put back down.

I looked over at Isabelle. She was giggling.

"What are you looking at?" exclaimed the others.

"Can't you see this guy?"

Isabelle kept giggling. Obviously, we were the only two who could. "Proud little fella, isn't he?"

As we walked away, quietly amused, the entity walked with me, still grasping my fingers.

Another perfectly normal day at the portal.

ALIENS VISIT THE MAYA

Juxtaposing manmade structures to mark and enhance natural portals reaches its apogee in the world of the Maya, particularly the sites in and around Guatemala. Temple cities such as Palenque and Tikal represent some of the most eloquent accomplishments of the stonemason's art. There is obvious passion in every movement of the chisel, in every expression of geometry, in every relationship between two blocks of limestone.

The Maya followed in the footsteps of the original builders, whom they describe as *Architects of the Sky*. They are said to have come from the stars and spoke He-Suyua-Thau, *the language of light.* Teachers such as Kinich-Muwaj, Chak-Tok-Ich-Aak, and Ix'Kalom-Te created temple cities where science, art, philosophy and religion formed a whole. The Mayan word for pyramid is *nah ku, house of the god,* which happens to be the name of the Egyptian *Aku,* the Shining Ones.

Should you find yourself at Tikal or Palenque after dark with a night watchman, he will tell you that the idea of the builder gods coming from the stars is not farfetched at all. On more than one occasion, a gentleman whom I shall refer to as Pablo X witnessed a spectacle both illuminating and frightening.

Pablo X is a quiet, humble man who lives in a small jungle village, a typical tight community bound by tradition, superstition, and religion. In other words, everyone knows everyone and everything that goes on in their personal lives. To step outside this social contract is to incur scorn, ridicule and, for really serious indiscretions, ostracism.

When someone experiences an otherworldly encounter, they are faced with two options: keep quiet or face exclusion from family and social life. Pablo X chose neither. He reluctantly chose to talk. But only under two conditions: he will share his experience after he befriends you and knows you are a person of honor, and two, you'll invent a fictitious name for him. Which I have.

Like every other night, Pablo X left home with a small bag of food to stop him feeling peckish, walked a few miles to Palenque, and took up his regular watchman position on the top platform of a pyramid from where he is afforded a wide view of the temple complex. If conditions are right, some nights bring out the *Aluxes*—elves, fairies or gods, nobody really knows, who are often helpful, even playful, but most of the time, bashful. Manifesting as small orbs of brightly colored light, they flit around the summits of hills and the canopy of tropical trees. "That," says Pedro X, "is really cool."

Then there are those rare occasions when a bright ball of light descends from the sky and hovers above the pyramids of Palenque before landing in the main plaza. "This one was the size of a very big house." The luminosity of the orb is such that it lights the detail in the surrounding buildings. It stretches here and there as though acclimating to its new reality before stabilizing. At this point, a gash-like opening appears in the fabric of the orb, the light gushing from within casting a yellowish beam on the grass of the plaza.

Moments later, a group of tall, oval shaped lights exit the orb and glide toward step pyramid XI. They come to a halt in front of its staircase, shrink, and transform into what appear to be humanoids wearing a kind of tight fitting, silver latex uniform. They gather to exchange some kind of communication before walking toward pyramid XI and literally enter the building as though it was nothing more than a translucent projected image.

Pablo X is paralyzed with a mixture of fear and wonder for a few minutes before calming himself and running down from his vantage point to meet the strangers. If they are pranksters, they'll be arrested; if it's a hallucination, it won't matter; if something else, well, we shall see...

He barely gets to within a hundred yards when one of the humanoids exits the pyramid, moves his hand in circular fashion and...the next thing Pablo X remembers is being unable to move. Even his vocal chords are paralyzed. Some time goes by before he watches the group return to the large orb, whereupon it rises and, at an astonishing rate of acceleration, vanishes into the starry sky.

His next recollection is waking up in his bed before dawn, fully clothed, and his wife with a scowl on her face, not because he might have done something daft like sleep in his work clothes but because he was home too early. Had he been fired, and if so, what were they going to do for food?

The following day, an article in the national newspaper described a possible violation of Guatemalan airspace by an unspecified bright light, witnessed by many village people around Palenque, prompting the air force to scramble a plane to investigate.

It seems we are back to where we began this adventure, with those *snakes whichsoever move along the Earth, which are in sky and heaven.* While we have been discussing portals as terrestrial pools of possibility—first among a virgin landscape and later harnessed within temples and other sacred places—the experience of Pablo X, along with those of Indigenous people and myself, suggests these places are also inter-dimensional access points linking multiple levels of reality.

A portal is a step into a thousand journeys.

PART TWO

*Energetic Doorways to Mystical
Experiences Between Worlds*

The experience of two worlds makes you present in both but bound to neither.

— FREDDY SILVA

THE WALL THAT IS NOT A WALL

n occasion, passage mounds became known in northern Europe as *giant's graves*, partly because of their association with very, very tall people, and sometimes because the remains of people up to 8.5 feet tall were buried in them, specifically skulls, tibias and forefingers, the bones shamans claim to contain the memory as well as the energy of their former owners.

I was spoiled whilst learning my trade in central Wiltshire, England, home of crop circles and sacred sites galore. I could take an afternoon walk and go write or meditate on any one of a dozen giant's graves, some within walking distance of my thatched cottage. In hindsight, it was compensation for the life of plenty I'd abandoned to follow the path I was meant to walk.

At the time I did not fully know how such temples functioned, if they did at all. I was driven by passion and a willingness to learn and walk through gates I never knew existed. More often than not, I returned with a virgin notepad, cursing the sky for wasting my life away as a hapless romantic of antiquities. The following day, verbs, adjectives and nouns poured out of me like a waterfall, and the information wouldn't stop until one o'clock in the morning. Eating became erratic at best. That's the moment you realize how portals work, and how each one is designed to elicit a certain process.

At one point I became the unofficial caretaker of a particular giant's grave that, together with five other mounds set among the bucolic landscape around Little Bedwyn, formed the mirror image of Lyre, the constellation associated with sound, as it had appeared in the sky some 6,000 years ago above Hampshire. The mound in question is protected by woods inside private land and receives no visitors I'm aware of, yet this portal is still quite active, for it is also protected by two entities that much resemble twenty-foot-tall stalks of bamboo. I couldn't believe what I was seeing. A whisper of wind sets them swaying from side to side; they have a very flute-like manner of speaking, expressed in low tones and slow diction. All perfectly understandable in English, naturally. *I don't know how they do it.* They resembled animated characters from a Miyazaki movie swaying in the breeze.

Every time I came to visit and boost the energy of the site we would have an amicable and slightly comical exchange. And it *was* comical… until I made my first visit to New Zealand.

The effects of four weeks of nonstop touring finally caught up with me just as I was being introduced to some very interesting people with a deep interest in the country's prehistory—the one modern Maori and European academics claim does not exist, in spite of overwhelming evidence to the contrary, particularly from the Maori themselves!

They wished to take me in a minibus to a site of significance. I wished to sleep. They left me to snooze for an hour or so, until I awoke with a sudden burst of energy.

"Are we headed toward the gap between those two hills?"

"Yes. How do you know, you've never been here?"

"I just got a big *whooomph* of energy coming from there," I replied.

They looked blankly at me. *Perhaps not a group who might appreciate this kind of vocabulary*, I thought, *best continue my nap.*

A while later, we stopped in the middle of a forest. The group was pointing excitedly to the right and made exclamations about something I couldn't quite make out. But my attention was taken to the left. I couldn't believe what I was seeing.

"What are you two doing here?" I asked.

"What are you pointing at?" asked the group.

"Those two figures over there!" Blank stares. "Give me a piece of paper and a pen. I'll draw them."

Two entities resembling twenty-foot-tall stalks of bamboo, swaying, with low, flute-like voices responded: *We're also responsible for this site.*

I was gobsmacked. *You have two jobs?*

Many. What brings you here?

Learning. Always.

One gentleman in the group remarked, "That's amazing."

"Not really," I said. "Anyone can develop this ability. You just become more sensitive to the environment around you."

"That's not what I mean. It's amazing because this drawing and your description are identical to those made by the last person we brought here, the dowser Hamish Miller."

"Hamish? Oh yes, he taught me dowsing. Came over for drinks last month," I replied.

Small universe.

And so we walked over to the oddly named Kaimanawa wall. Odd because it resembles a two-tier wall of megaliths, but on close inspection, it appears to be a kind of truncated pyramid. Much of the site is concealed under layers of ash deposited by active volcanoes forty miles away.

A surreptitious trench dug alongside the visible layer of megaliths clearly shows a set of manmade blocks beneath. Perfectly preserved by ash, they look as though sliced by laser, expertly fitted, with joints so fine it is impossible to insert a kiwi feather between them. The floor of the five-foot-deep hole is a paper-flat monolith.

I jump in, and to my astonishment, an echo booms from below. There's a hollow chamber under there. There's a room. But what makes this place a portal?

Standing at the summit, an energy upwells like a vortex, and it burns up my spine with the subtlety of an acetylene torch. It is palpable to everyone in the group. It seems the Kaimanawa wall is in fact an *ahu,* a type of step platform found throughout the Pacific, and specifically on Easter Island, where groups of sages nicknamed Shining Ones used to gather in conclave in the remote past.

For the first time that day, I was awake.

Freddy Silva

THE ASDUISDI

*I*n the summer of 1936, a few months after their marriage, my parents bought a log cabin built in the 1850s in rural North Carolina. As was the custom of that time, family and friends traveled from far and wide to celebrate their wonderful new home, bringing enough food and supplies for an extended stay.

My maternal great-great-grandmother, Keziah Rose, traveled from the foothills of the Blue Ridge Mountains to attend the celebration. Keziah Rose was full-blooded Cherokee Indian, a seer, fire-talker, midwife, root doctor, and the family's beloved matriarch.

Soon after her arrival, Keziah performed a white sage smudging ritual to purify the cabin and the surrounding property. Upon completing the ritual, she promptly announced that she had found an *asduisdi*—the Cherokee word for portal or gateway—in a low-lying area in the backyard. The family was aware of Keziah's ability to sense Elohi's (Earth's) spirit energy and greeted the announcement with excitement and joy, followed by three days of celebration under the shade of the ancient black locust tree that grew beside the asduisdi.

My mother was the seventh daughter of a seventh daughter, a significant sign of power and fortune within her Native American family. From a young age, she exhibited the same prophetic and healing abilities as her great-grandmother, Keziah. But after moving to the log cabin, her powers became significantly stronger than those of Keziah, and she credited the asduisdi as the source of her enhanced abilities.

I became aware of my connection to this powerful source a few weeks before my sixth birthday when I contracted a severe case of measles. I was so ill that my parents decided to move me into their bedroom so they could sit vigil at my bedside.

By the third day of the illness, I developed a high fever and was in and out of consciousness, barely able to see through my half-opened eyes. I heard them speak in low, hushed voices as they placed cold cloths on my forehead.

I sensed fear in their whispers, and I became frightened and asked them, "Am I going to die?"

My dad embraced me and said, "You will be fine," as he laid me gently back down upon the pillow.

Settling in, I opened my eyes and saw the ceiling above me slowly disappear, replaced by the most brilliant blue I had ever seen. It was a sky dotted with fluffy white clouds, and from amidst the clouds, a hand reached out to me.

Sitting up, I took the hand and left my physical body, my parents, and my home far behind. I held onto the hand as tightly as I could and was pulled faster and faster through the clouds toward a beautiful white light. As I entered the light, it gradually dissipated. Still holding onto the hand that had reached out to me from the clouds, I looked up and saw the familiar face of a man. I could not recall how I knew him, but the love and kindness radiating from his face awakened a bond that filled me with warmth and security. The brilliant, white light that shimmered around his body caused me to gasp with reverence.

The man smiled down at me and gestured with a sweeping wave of his hand, suggesting that we walk forward onto a deeply worn path. The path ran through the middle of an ancient village. On either side of the path were mud-brick houses, each with an enclosed area marked by weather-worn stone pillars and carefully placed timbers. Within the confines of each enclosure, colorful flowers grew alongside plants and trees while livestock grazed nearby. In the distance, I could see a wall surrounding the village constructed of stones in different shapes and sizes, overgrown with ropy vines that broke down the stone in some places.

Villagers—brown-skinned men, women, and children—were tending the gardens, caring for the animals, and cheerfully talking and laughing with one another. It was a beautiful and blissful scene. My eyes locked with theirs, and I sensed a soul-level connection to these people, a deep and meaningful bond that went back many lifetimes.

When I peered into the face of the celestial being, he nodded in acknowledgment, confirming my connection to these people. And with that nod, I awoke to find myself in the physical world, lying in my parents' bed. They were standing over me and began to cry as I regained consciousness. They scooped me up into their arms and held me tightly.

I felt disappointed and saddened to be back in the physical world, in my tiny body, wracked by fever and chills. But I was also happy because I knew something special had happened to me that day. My near-death journey to the ancient village was just the beginning of numerous spiritually transformative experiences that occurred during my youth at the cabin on the grounds of the asduisdi.

Pamela Nance

STEPPING INTO THE FIRE

*M*y face is frozen with the chill of daybreak. Biting gusts of wind snatch strands of hair from beneath my woolly hat, whipping my eyes awake. I wonder why I'm not snug in my bed. Huffing through my knitted gloves, warming my hands before shoving them back in my pockets, I nod at the stone giants of Kura Tawhiti that tower over me. They are wearing hats of snow.

The silvery light shivering between the enormous stones brings some cheer. Like long, bony fingers of the ancient gods who once dwelt here, these first uncertain rays reach into crevices and crannies to discover who has appeared among them on this wintry solstice day.

"I would kill for a coffee," I mutter to those in earshot.

Our matronly facilitator hears our muffled giggles. "No talking please," she scolds, making us want to laugh louder.

Snow crunches and sighs under our boots as we slowly wend our way through the labyrinth of soaring stones, guided by torchlight. I'm relieved that our gathering point is sheltered as I find my place among twelve companions shuffling into a circle around the altar, their faces flamingo pink with cold. This is not like a church altar, but an oblong-shaped slab of limestone that rests on the ground. Two women light tall candles inside glass lanterns, placing them alongside several crystals. Another arranges a garland of flowers and ferns, and another light cones of incense. I am a relative newbie, but I take it all in.

It's 2010, ten years since my teen son died; a completion for Tim but a beginning for me, for it was the departure of his physical form that opened the door to the non-physical world. Until then, I would have visited Castle Hill, as it's also known, to clamber over the curiously shaped rocks or throw a rope and hook into a fissure to scamper up for a glorious view of the Southern Alps. But over time, my inner work through the journey of grief has changed all that. Tim is now one of my guides.

Many in our group speak about rare vibrational frequencies and energies experienced here, which some New Zealanders consider to be their country's "heart chakra." I discreetly ask the woman next to me if it's true the Dalai Lama made a pilgrimage here. She nods, not wanting to be glared at by our stern leader. But at an opportune moment, she whispers, "He described Kura Tawhiti as a great spiritual center of the universe. He even called it his second home."

I gaze over at the women and men who can see nature spirits, angelics, and orbs of light, wishing I could do the same. Although I communicate telepathically with my beloved son, I am not gifted with special sight. I sometimes feel insecure and less spiritually developed because of this and have become obsessed with seeing beyond the veil into the world of spirit. My expectations are high at Kura Tawhiti.

Our facilitator reins in my wistful thoughts by invoking the *kaitiaki*, the guardians and keepers of wisdom at this sacred site. Her high, reedy voice is thinned by the cold and barely audible, yet there is no doubt of her sincerity.

"We come in peace, in the spirit of oneness, seeking permission to commune with the ancient ones, the Stone People. We have come to connect with the wisdom of these unseen teachers and are grateful for this opportunity."

Standing ankle-deep in snow, my poor feet painfully cold, it's hard to focus on ancient gods. Remembering I'm in a stone library holding rare knowledge, I push thoughts of chilblains aside and concentrate, marveling how this library is not accessed with a bar code but through an open heart and mind.

One of the women chants an incantation to help us forget our discomfort and enter the portals of our hearts. At first, I'm distracted, but I gradually move away from my physical state into a higher level of consciousness. The energies are palpable; I feel them as pressure on my chest and slowness of breath. I peer through my eyelashes for a moment to watch curling tendrils of mist spiraling in front of my face. I breathe deeper. Slower. Silence roars in my ears like a rush of wind.

Then all is peaceful—but not for long.

I'm vaguely aware that my feet are warming up. *How curious, and what a blessing*, I think.

The warmth builds, intensifying into heat. It's as though someone is stoking a furnace beneath the Earth. The soles of my feet are on fire now, and I lift one foot and then the other as though the snow will put out the blaze. I'm aware of the chafing noise that my parka is making as I hop about like silver on a smithy's forge. I open my eyes aghast to see our leader frowning at me. My feet are burnt toast. Bewildered, I take my boots off and stand in the snow in stocking feet, but this makes no difference at all. How I long for frozen toes and chilblains now!

After what seems an agonizingly long time, others begin to stretch their bodies as they return from their journeys. A talking stick is passed around the circle and each of us speaks of our experience. Some describe fantastic visions of cosmic beings shimmering in gold, while others proclaim profound insights.

Dreading my turn, I take the stick in both hands and begin by apologizing. "I'm sorry for my distracting behavior. It sounds weird, but my feet were scorching. I felt as though my feet were Sunday's roast."

Chortles ripple around the group. When it is calm again, to my surprise, I discover that I know what occurred. Without hesitating, I tell them, "It was Gaia sending up energies from her core. She has activated the chakras in the soles of my feet for future work. She says that in the years to come, I will travel to her sacred sites around the planet to activate portals that have cycles of activity and dormancy."

Brushing away tears, I share the second part of her message. "She's asking me to understand that I'm not a visual seer, but that I have other gifts. She says I see with my feelings and my body."

I feel Tim's presence behind me and hear him say, *Nice work, Mumsy. Another beginning.*

Making my way back to the lodge for hot drinks and breakfast, I'm brimming with excitement. A young woman falls in beside me and pushes her hood back, her dark eyes bright as she says, "I'm so glad you shared your story. I have often felt disappointed when not seeing. Today, I realized I have the same gifts as you."

A few weeks later, an email arrives with a photograph attached. One member of our group, a professional photographer, had been shaken out of his meditation and was prompted to take a shot while the rest of us were still journeying. In this photograph, not one person is recognizable. All that can be seen in the numinous light of Kura Tawhiti suspended between night and day, is a sphere of golden lights and tall white flames.

Annwyn

THE MOTHER PORTAL AT BANDELIER

*M*ost of the tourists had gone home that summer evening. The park would be closing soon, but I wanted a little more time to sit in meditation in one of the cliff hollows made accessible by a modern-day ladder.

This site, known as the *Tyuonyi Pueblo,* is part of the Bandelier National Monument near Los Alamos, New Mexico. About 800 years ago, a tribe of Puebloans settled near the creek at the base of towering cliffs of sedimentary rock and compressed volcanic ash known as *Bandelier Tuff.* They built homes out of carved rock and mud bricks, an interconnected jumble of rooms three levels high. Their main village was constructed around the perimeter of a circle that embraced an open yard and a kiva dug into the earth. In the cliffs that rose above the settlement on the canyon floor, they dug rooms, or *cavates*, in the softer layers of Tuff. Today we don't know if these rooms were living or working spaces or used for ritual.

I felt fortunate to be at the pueblo sitting cross-legged on the sandy floor at the cliff-face opening of one of the interconnected rooms, where I could look out over the majestic rock formations and the circular ruins far below. The space dug into the cliff wall, which many people climb into and out of on any typical day, was not tall enough for me to stand in. This particular *cavate* was a series of three interconnected spaces with smoke stains on the ceiling and niches dug into the walls.

I looked around the dwelling and wondered how the people who had created this space might have used the little carved-out shelves. I imagined a child keeping treasured trinkets or a parent storing special tools or food. I tried to imagine what it would be like to shelter here with a warm fire burning, to live a life working or sleeping in a cave high above the valley floor. I allowed myself to drift into a drowsy, dreamy state.

The wind picked up, chilling me. Although I was sheltered from the worst of it, I pulled my collar up around my neck. The sky was filling with typical, New Mexican afternoon monsoon clouds. They were dark and ominous as they barreled in my direction. I could see lightning. The booms of thunder were sounding closer and closer. I knew I would have to leave soon if I was going to stay dry, but something urged me to sit there quietly, just a little longer.

As I looked down again over the village ruins, I imagined the families who had once lived there. It was dinnertime and the weather was threatening. I know I would have been calling my kids inside. Down in the valley, I imagined I could hear the young mothers calling out to their children.

"Come on in. It'll be raining soon. Come eat your dinner."

I could almost smell the food cooking in hive-like *fornos* or over open fires. The mothers would be urgently waving.

"Come in. Now!"

I could hear the children laughing and calling like my own children had, saying goodbye to their friends and throwing their balls one last time, reluctant to stop their play.

I felt a flood of gratitude for these young mothers and the effort they made to care for their families. To feed the children and make sure they had clothes. Ancient mothers had held humanity together. On the backs of those women, we have created the privilege to participate in the 21st century.

Wave after wave of gratitude and appreciation brought tears to my eyes. I reached out to these young mothers from my heart. *I see you. I understand what you feel. I have felt it too. You cannot see it now, but your love for your children and your tribe has made my life, far in your future, possible. It is hard for you to understand now, but you are an important thread in a tapestry that stretches far beyond all that you will know. Your motherhood thread carries the love and hope that keep humanity sane. I am grateful. I am grateful. I am grateful.*

I felt outside of time as I sat in a trance of appreciation—as if I were there, hearing and seeing the activity in the village below me. I gradually became aware of a pulling sensation in my back between my shoulder blades. It was like someone was pulling on my sweater, and I felt—more than heard—a shimmering voice echoing the words that I had been thinking.

I realized that I was sitting in a portal, a mother portal, a through-line of energy that stretched through innumerable generations into my past and future. A future mom was extending to me the love and encouragement I was attempting to extend to the ancient moms of the ruined village below.

My body shivered. I could feel it all, the past, present, and future all tied together in an ecstatic field of mutual appreciation and love. It was an outside-of-time sharing of experiences: giving birth, caring for infants and children, the weariness of housework, the joy of watching the children learn and grow, and sometimes, the indescribable pain of loss.

I have always imagined that I honored motherhood and its searing process of loving beyond comprehension, working beyond exhaustion, and fearing beyond measure. In my experience, moms don't usually allow themselves to feel how important they are; they are too busy facing the next task, the next need to be met, the next challenge. On that chilly afternoon, embraced in ancient rock, I was able to both give and receive a sense of understanding and being understood, of validating and honoring as well as being validated and honored.

This experience touched me on a profound level. I imagine that some of those ancient moms looked up toward the cliff, just for a second, on that blustery day and felt the love and appreciation that flowed through that portal. I know that sometime, somewhere in the future, living in a world that I cannot imagine, there is a woman contemplating the journey of motherhood, and that she is connected with my heart and loving and appreciating me and my journey as well.

Sue Bryan, Ph.D.

SKELLIG MICHAEL

"**B**e careful as you make it all the way up to the monastery. It's very wet and steep," Dermott cautioned. "We've had fatalities."

Swallowing hard, I fastened the strap of my camera bag tightly around my waist as if it could somehow keep me from falling to my death from the jagged cliff in front of us. After I jumped from the tiny fishing boat to the small, wet landing, my feet planted—if not securely, at least fully—on Skellig Michael. Before me stretched the six hundred loose stone steps that would carry me up 700 feet above the Atlantic Ocean. The idea filled me with excitement and fear.

I'd seen documentaries about the tragic deaths of visitors who had slipped and tumbled to their deaths there. My family, even Dermott, had warned me about the danger. But the words of the proprietress of the bed and breakfast we had stayed in Kenmare rang louder: "If you have a mind to do it, then you must."

Placing one foot upon the stone step in front of me, I began my ascent. My legs shook as I carefully put one foot in front of the other, ignoring the sheer drop-off on both sides. Nothing was there to catch me if I stumbled. I would fall straight into the cold, dark ocean surrounding this tiny island.

Puffins perched here and there along the path, completely unaware of the challenge this climb presented to me. Their presence was comforting as they basked in the unusually warm Irish sun. But I didn't want to be distracted, so I turned my focus back to the stone slabs.

I stopped briefly to catch my breath at the rock formation known as the Wailing Woman. The top of the rock shaped like a woman turned toward the sea, watching over the souls lost there or endlessly waiting for one to come back. The awe-inspiring beauty surrounding me took from me what little breath I had left. I was struck by the strength, determination, and fortitude of the monks who laid these steps one by one and then built the village I would be rewarded to see when I reached the top.

Standing where they stood thousands of years ago, looking out to the sea, I felt the energy shift. I could almost see them slowly, meditatively walking up with me. Taking these steps as my own pilgrimage, I was trying to work out the worldly and the spiritual so they could coexist peacefully within me. Knowing the monks had done this, I felt less alone and more connected to myself and this other world.

Slowly and mindfully, I continued to climb while the winding path grew narrow until the ground before me flattened. A grassy path took me to the stone doorway leading to the village. I dared to glance down. Boats like dots speckled the ocean, and birds brought my eyes back up to the sky, the heavens.

"I'm here," I whispered, proud of my achievement.

The sacred energy enveloped and welcomed me as I stepped through the doorway. The village, the monks' refuge built so long ago, was still vibrant and alive with their spirits. Nothing appeared to have deteriorated or decayed. Instead, it was as it had always been.

Beehive huts lined the outer walls of the village. The monastery just ahead of me and the graveyard on my left vibrated with the lives that farmed, worshipped, lived, and died here. As I found my way to a beehive hut along the back wall, I noticed my steps were softer and less deliberate than on my climb, as if I was afraid to disturb those who still lingered.

The curved door opened into a dark, dome-like structure. The darkness contrasted the brilliant sunshine outside, and I had to wait for my eyes to adjust. Standing in total darkness, I felt neither here nor there, suspended in some in-between place. Shapes formed before me; shadows moved in the space around me. I was not afraid.

I watched and then slowly sat on the cool, dirt floor. No light made its way through these rocks stacked centuries ago. I could smell smoke from their fires and hear the wind lashing rain against the outer stone walls that kept the inside dry and almost warm. Shadows danced in the flickering light as the inhabitants went about their daily activities. A straw mat on the floor provided a bed for those who would shelter there for the night. I reached out, unsure if I could touch the shadowy figures.

Have I entered a dream?

The beings acted as if they had been expecting me. My body relaxed on the ground as a wave of peace and calm moved through me. Connection. Belonging. I was one with them, myself, with everything. I felt whole in a way I had never experienced.

"Excuse me."

I jumped at the voice behind me as a young couple entered the beehive hut.

"Oh, sorry. I didn't see you there," I admitted, scrambling to my feet, and moving out into the brightness of the day. My legs were a little wobbly.

How long was I there? I wondered as I adjusted to being in the bright sun again.

After several minutes, with legs more able and willing, I climbed up the grassy hill just outside the village walls and sat. The warm sun held me as if I were wrapped in a blanket, and I breathed in the fresh air. People milled about, exploring the village, yet I felt alone. Tears wet my eyes with a deep knowing, a deep connection, love.

Noticing a line of people starting to descend the steps, I realized there was little time before I had to be back at the boat. I pushed myself up from the grass and walked back into the village, slowly passing the huts and rock-walled garden of the monastery, taking in and sharing energies. The graveyard drew my attention, and I stood looking over the stones that marked lives lost. My hand reached down, pulling up three small pebbles, and I reverently placed them in my pocket. They would serve as a reminder of this time, an assurance that I would never forget this sacred experience.

Skellig Michael had changed me.

Mary-Elizabeth Briscoe

A THOUSAND YEARS TELLING

*A*s if called by some holy messenger, we traveled through purple skies across the wide Pacific, following an endless setting sun. It was the year 2000 when the world was teetering on the start of a new millennium full of promise. Soon after my arrival on the other side of the world—expectant, wide-eyed—I began to hear the portal's hum.

I was on a journey from Atlanta with other Qi Gong and Tai Chi students of Master Chen, a Taoist priest of Wudang. He had been trained from childhood by elder Taoist masters and was now in the United States to fulfill a mission, his master's vision. It was time, she had declared, to bring this ancient knowledge and spiritual practice to the West. This sacred wisdom, gathered in stillness by closely observing the universe for thousands of years, was about to be shared. Our travels in China, therefore, took a more mystical path.

Our first bit of mysticism surrounded meeting that visionary, our teacher's revered master, Grandmaster Chen Li—a life that had touched three centuries. At 128 years old, she was the highest-level Taoist and leader—a future Immortal. It was her spirit that brought me on this journey. My adventure would prove what poets and shamans have long known: seeking beauty cracks open a gracious heart.

China is a vast country, and the Taoists are tucked away high in the remote Wudang Mountains. After traveling by local plane, long bus rides, an overnight train, and more winding bus rides, we arrived at the renowned Purple Cloud Temple in Wudang—where masters still train in the healing art of Taoist Tai Chi. We watched as they moved rhythmically, powerfully, almost magically, across the ancient stone courtyard. The hum was strong and steady.

The mountain peaks called to us. After a spectacular cable car ride to the highest peak and its Golden Palace, considered the soul of the mountain, we were first greeted by the tall skeleton of an old tree starkly silhouetted in the mist. It was like a sentinel posted here to protect a hallowed gateway, its bare branches reaching out to bless us. I paused, listening. We walked on to the sacred enclave, small temples built in elegant harmony with nature, poised on the narrow mountaintop so high that with every breath we inhaled and exhaled clouds.

I closed my eyes for a moment, feeling the deep resonance of this majestic place, then I turn and come face-to-face with a grandfatherly priest, his long gray beard circling around his feet. He bowed and traded us blessed brass coins for a promise I no longer remember, but the telling hum of the skeleton tree stayed with me.

As some of the first Westerners to visit this remarkable Taoist landscape, listening to stories of its historic lineage, we felt the privilege of the invitation. When it was time to meet Grandmaster Chen Li, we were deeply aware of the honor.

The beloved teacher lived with four elder priestesses in a modest, three-structure compound built at the far end of a large, burnt-out courtyard—once part of an emperor's summer palace. Massive bronze statues remain as a reminder of its forgotten grandeur. A series of stone steps and crumbling border walls gave a sense of its immense scale where long ago 5,000 warriors trained at one time. But now, a thousand years on, this cherished place reverberated with something more powerful and everlasting: the wisdom and prescience of a woman of vision.

After a welcoming ceremonial ritual by young priestesses—chanting and swirling in their chrysanthemum brocade—the grandmaster quietly greeted us dressed in her formal silk robes and simple headdress. Invited inside her small dwelling our joy filled the space and the hum grew stronger, more visceral in her presence. She chatted softly and affectionately with Chen, who sat close to her, sharing his master's greetings with these visitors from a faraway world. And for those who could hear, the once ineffable was being revealed. I left her knowing something essential had shifted within me. I had crossed a threshold.

Our traveling continued and I felt as if being drawn toward something holy. Along the way, music and dance entertained us, expanding our sensibilities. We enjoyed a lyrical performance of the traditional long-sleeve folk dance. As the women swayed and dipped, gracefully swinging their flowing sleeves, moving in a hypnotic rhythm, the Divine Feminine emerged.

We floated on the Yangtze River, a cruise through the mythic Three Gorges, and the hum became even more musical, more sensual. We were serenaded with the pure sounds of the fabled stringed gupin, its transcendent tones lifting me into what I experienced as a new dimension of awareness.

After a day's bus ride along the Min River Canyon, we arrived at dusk in paradise. Nestled between mountains on the edge of the Tibetan Plateau, the secluded Jiuzhaigou Valley—full of luxuriant forests, pristine lakes, and endless waterfalls—had been unknown to the outside world until the 1970s. This natural wonderland has been recognized as a nature reserve and national park to protect the beauty that Mother Nature creates when left to her own exuberant devices. And now it was October when she goes mad with color.

When in the thick of nature—especially in a forest with old-growth lushness—my senses seem to catch on my breath, and the air quivers like it's carrying coded messages from the Mother Trees. Here in Jiuzhaigou—the hum pulsating, the portal closer, and the air ripe—a sacred, sensory feast awaited me.

I was constantly aware of the aliveness of nature here, energized by the surrounding sound and feel of moving waters. Water is the spiritual heart of the valley; lakes, springs, waterfalls, rivers, and shoals formed by waters pouring down from the snow-capped peaks merged, sometimes roaring into each other. Other waters were so quiet and tranquil; stillness became a reverie.

There was a liminal quality to this valley where broadleaf trees and scented conifers grow together at the very spot where the southern and northern vegetation regions join. I stared into hillsides scattered with evergreens, October-colored hardwoods, and golden trees—cypresses perhaps—that looked like luminous angel wings. They were brightly lit even on cloudy days, as though a giant strobe had blasted the mountainside. And with a magician's flair, that abundance is reflected in the clear, still, mineral-rich waters of a hundred azure-blue lakes.

Color can have such an emotional, imaginative impact. Blue—perhaps because nature surrounds us with it in the sky and sea—can bring reassuring calm and spiritual openings. The stories of the color's mythology touch on the Divine. In Jiuzhaigou, shades of blue run through the sacred, sometimes playing tricks with our senses. Peacock River, vivid and iridescent, runs into Colorful Lake whose clear waters blended shades of turquoise and jade and lapis lazuli, displaying beautiful, jeweled patterns formed by fallen trees immersed for hundreds of years.

Walking around its banks, we discovered an enchanted little forest of pine and aspen trees on a gentle slope where the root formations twisted into perfect homes for pixies and gnomes. Huge rocks blanketed in dense moss and exotic ferns—emphasizing the primordial character of this place—looked as if giant green yaks had dropped to the forest floor, then left in peaceful, ageless slumber. The hum felt seductive, enveloping, warm. I yearned to curl up and lose myself here, to dream heroic stories, reimagining the first time I lived in paradise.

Visiting one of Jiuzhaigou's many waterfalls, we walked across Pearl Shoals on a boardwalk built a few feet above the fast-moving, dancing waters that would soon crash over rocks, falling into streams far below. Master Chen stopped us in the middle of the walkway to feel the energy and hear the waters' sounds, to pay attention to the gentle, staccato rhythm before it was drowned out by the falls, becoming part of the crescendo. When we reached the far side of the shallows, we began our misty descent on steps built at the very edge of the falls—its roar enveloping me. I felt I was inside its resounding yet intimate power.

At times during our bus rides around this winding valley, I pondered the nature of mirage. I kept seeing a white horse, large and regal, grazing in the same spot in a meadow of tall grass each time we passed by. Were we going in circles, or was I seeing it for the first time, not remembering I had dreamed of it before? Dreams and reality become topsy-turvy in paradise.

On our last day, we set out to explore more of the valley, and I lagged behind the group, not wanting to miss one speck of beauty. During one of these dawdling moments, I stopped to read a sign near the smooth trunk of an undistinguished old tree: "*Sabina ehinzensis,* 1,000-year-old pine. Many grow this old here." I stared in awe. I knew I was a bit intoxicated from absorbing so many splendors during the last several days, but this information unraveled me.

Where I grew up in the river woodlands of Alabama, we considered a pine tree that grew to 100 years old an old tree. As I stood on the ground far from my childhood home, staring at this ancient pine in a remote valley in China, I remembered how my grandfather and father spoke about walking through those woods, amongst magnificent trees, like they were in church. This was hallowed ground.

I continued to stand at the foot of this lone pine tree, weeping. I saw Master Chen further down the path, looking back at me—he nodded in recognition. I could no longer contain the hum; my longing surrendered, cracking open all that I thought was possible. A vibration moved through me into what was no longer just a tree, but a view into another dimension. Through my tears, I could see the face of Grandmaster Chen Li in the tree's gray patina, and she spoke to me without words. My body seemed to dissolve, and my face merged with hers, with all the Immortals, with all the wise ones of the universe, most not of this Earth. I saw beyond seeing, heard beyond hearing—their loving messages carried in currents of long waves that stretched me into the future of human consciousness.

After moments, or perhaps lifetimes, I came back into my body. My cells felt somehow rearranged. I instinctively shuddered as if to recalibrate this new universe inside me. The old tree was still in front of me, a ghostly light shimmering through her faded trunk—a signal, perhaps, for future kindred spirits who might come along this path, led here by a mysterious hum.

Something now feels shared, whole, and divinely guided. This fresh awareness moves with me into the forest where wild things speak, and I write down their stories. As with the ancient Taoists, the stories awaken our imagination and curiosity, touch our inner being, and move us into stillness. With this view into a new future, this long-awaited fulfillment, original stories are coming through to connect us and draw us together as one. They will serve as a pathway leading us all home, separate no more.

Cornelia Powell

INTERDIMENSIONAL KAIMANAWA FOREST

While driving the Napier-Taupo highway in New Zealand, I felt a force pulling my heart and throat chakra in the direction of a forest some distance away. Sharing my story with a friend, I learned I had been near the mysterious Kaimanawa Wall. Because Taupo was my place of birth, I innately knew this held great significance for me.

The wall drew me so powerfully that I couldn't resist, and as much as my "monkey mind" tried to talk me out of it, I found the courage to seize this opportunity to find this wall shrouded in great mystery.

With no real clarity on exactly where it was, I began my journey into the Kaimanawa forest. I set the intention to be gifted a small rock from around the wall if I was allowed one.

Petrified and crying, my anxiety levels were through the roof as I drove alone into a densely canopied, stunning rainforest guided only by Source and this monument I was about to meet.

Arriving at the wall the energy felt like a high-powered electric plant. As I stepped out of my car, I collapsed in an unfathomable surge of both grief and gratitude for being there again. In a spontaneous, altered state, I picked up a random, small rock on the path and sobbed out the words: "I have tried for so long to get back here."

Standing, I pressed my palms and forehead against the wall. With eyes closed, I basked in its sheer power and in the pure white energy beginning to form around me was transported back to a lifetime I had once lived in that spot.

I was no longer myself but a blue-skinned feline being with high priestess energy wearing an Egyptian headdress and elaborate jewelry. I became aware of three *patupaiarehe kaitiaki* (the guardian fairy folk of New Zealand forests) descending downhill toward me, curious about my intentions. I reassured them I was there for a good purpose, and they acknowledged the mutual respect we shared.

Reluctant to leave and promising to return, I started my journey home. The small rock I was gifted from the area in front of the Kaimanawa wall sat on my lap. As I drove along, it started to communicate with me. Taking a closer look, I realized it was no ordinary rock. I had, in fact, been gifted a piece of the wall itself that had fractured off.

Honoring the shamanic art of "a gift for a gift," my work with the Kaimanawa wall continues. I have since met others who also remembered spiritually elevated past lives at that location in its original, ancient structure and function. Sharing my story and teaching people about the wall has helped them remember who they are and their own infinite spiritual potential.

Ivy Megan

THE CELESTIAL REVERIE OF LAHILAHI

Since my early childhood, I have felt that I don't quite belong in this world. This feeling was intensified by my immigration from Hong Kong to the middle of nowhere Canada at the awkward age of ten. It became even stronger during my spiritual awakening as a lawyer at a large insurance firm.

Feeling like a misfit has led me to seek out places that hold a deeper, interconnected meaning. This quest has become a sacred key that opens doorways to places where time and physical space are formless concepts. Interdimensional realms that are accessible only to those who've realized that our so-called reality and identities are as fleeting as a ghostly image on an old TV screen.

A decade ago, I relocated to the island of Oahu, Hawaii. Traditional Hawaiian spiritual practices are based on their connection to their ancestral roots. The local people guard these treasured, sacred inheritances and rarely reveal them to those beyond the lineage. So far, the opportunity to unlock these legacies eluded me.

Kapu is the ancient Hawaiian code of conduct that includes many laws and regulations. In most cases, I don't know which spiritual practices or sacred sites are off-limits (*kapu*). I hold my own code of conduct to honor and respect all places, regardless of significance and allow that to preside over my fear of inadvertently crossing boundaries or offending wrathful deities. I choose to enter every place, labeled as sacred or not, silently and with an open heart. My senses will indicate if access is not being granted. All places are tended by their own guardian spirits with their own stories. We can't hear them if we are narrating at the same time.

Mauna Lahilahi or Lahilahi beckoned to my soul. Its name translates to "thin mountain" and conjures the image of its razor-like appearance. Its immediate neighbor is the Waianae Mountain Range, the eroded remains of an ancient shield volcano that boasts lush, undulating silhouettes reminiscent of majestic dragons. The highest peak on Oahu is there. At its feet lay the sharp-edged, rugged, and barren high rock of Lahilahi.

On an evening in March of 2021, I was watching the sunset when I heard Lahilahi's golden-sheened, jagged visage call out to me. I interrupted my two beach companions' idle chatter about their condo neighbors with a sense of urgency.

"Lahilahi is calling. I have to go."

Until that moment, I had never explored Lahilahi. As I was leaving, one of my friends mentioned that it is known as a sacred site.

Compelled by an invisible magnetism, I climbed halfway up the rugged cliffs. When I came across faint petroglyphs etched into the rock surface—symbols of four-legged animals and humans—my senses of their ancient life stories awakened. I saw that the shoreline below harbored large stones in other-worldly shapes. I wondered whether they had been strategically positioned to mark something important, and by whom.

What instantly struck me about Lahilahi, in addition to its 237-foot elevation, was the panoramic view it provided, even just at the halfway point. I imagined that I was a knight atop an ancient castle guarding the Waianae

Range, the expanse of the surrounding ocean, and the hustle and bustle of the Waianae suburb.

As the sky dimmed, I climbed back down to quickly explore a few of the stone structures that encircled Lahilahi. These might have been religious sites, burial sites, or *heiau* (temples). Tents had been interwoven between these sites. I waved hello to a couple of the residents. The more I tuned into the rocks, the more intensified my energetic field became. A flat, round stone no larger than a king-sized pillow magnetically lured me. Spontaneously, I removed my slippers and stood upon it to connect with its energetic field and the planetary grids below.

From this newfound vantage point, I found myself nestled in an alcove, gazing at the Waianae ridgeline. An inexplicable urge overcame me, and I began to tone. The resonance filled the air, and Lahilahi, once a mountain, now felt like the sacred walls of an ancient temple. I let the notes and breath transcend, carrying them to the undulating ridgeline and across the vast ocean. I felt the spirits awaken as twilight descended.

Promising to return, I left that sacred space, not expecting that Lahilahi had more in store for me that very night. I woke up to find myself in a dance, with movements resembling *hula*, which is not merely a dance in Hawaii but a form of storytelling through movements and gestures. I was in a semi-conscious state, on an interdimensional expedition. These spirits had chosen to tell me their story through a sacred dance. There was no music—just energy. My fingers and hands flowed in a cocoon of the viscous energies of another realm, while my physical form lay on my bed. In between waking and dreaming, I clearly saw myself standing at a *heiau* at Lahilahi.

A profound sense of love and connection enveloped me. Although unseen, these spirits guided my visions through Lahilahi's surroundings. I was given a VIP tour of Lahilahi's entire circumference; I recognized the large stones I'd seen earlier and learned of the stones' significant placements. Certain peaks of the Waianae lined up with dedicated stars. They were guiding stars, I was shown, not just for navigation but for spiritual knowledge and protection.

The *heiau*, once mysterious and undefined, now appeared dedicated to constellations, where a sacred dance was performed in reverence—a harmonious energy exchange, balancing the masculine and feminine. I continued to dance with the spirits and to worship the sky. Silent communion prevailed, and with each stone's alignment, I knew what they had felt when gazing upon aligned stars. The spirits worshiped the constellations, revealing how they mirrored the land's natural formations as if the celestial sky served as Earth's blueprint for elemental architects.

Time held no meaning during these moments, which spanned from the moon's zenith to the sun's rising. At my journey's end, I was gifted with a profound vision: an inner map summarizing all the alignments between stones, mountain peaks, and constellations. They wished me to grasp a grander perspective, a memory of seeing the world through their eyes.

Over the following days, I spent time researching Lahilahi's significance to ancient Hawaiians. One legend spoke of *The Story of Aiai*, where altars, stones, and enclosures marked various fishing grounds. Another tied the mountain to Kane, the god of protection and a principal Hawaiian deity.

There is little recorded knowledge about Lahilahi as a sanctuary for the stories of star worshipers, those who understand the constellations as the blueprint of our origins. Their sacred dance embodied an exchange of energy with the cosmos and a way to honor the stars. This knowledge was my sacred inheritance—for some secrets are meant for fellow misfits holding the sacred key.

Julie Suen

ENCOUNTER AT NEWGRANGE

*O*n a fine afternoon in October, a group of us entered the Newgrange passage tomb at Brú na Bóinne, Ireland. This Neolithic monument dates back to 3200 BC and is 249 feet wide and about 39 feet high, covering a little more than an acre of ground.

Like the nearby companion mounds of Knowth and Douth, Newgrange seems to have functioned as more than just a burial site. The structures might also have served as observatories of the heavens and keepers of stone calendars to record the movement and position of the luminaries.

The large kerbstones that ring these structures are carved fantastically with stars, dot patterns, the Moon, meanders, spirals, lozenges, and various serpent shapes, all of which have been associated with the continental cult of Magna Mater, which dates to about 9000 BC. The zig-zag patterns that are thought to symbolize water, life force, sound, and vibration might be more than 40,000 years old.

The entrance on the southeastern side of Newgrange is immediately fronted by a huge stone carved with swirls and lozenges. A sixty-foot, stone-lined passage runs about a third of the way into the center, and at the end are three smaller chambers going off from a large, central room. The cruciform layout is quite like that of the star constellation Cygnus the swan—not exactly symmetrical and similar in reflecting the position of key stars that define that constellation. Each of the smaller chambers has a large, flat basin stone where offerings may have been deposited. The main passageway is oriented exactly so that the winter solstice sun of 5,000 years ago would shine directly through a skybox placed above the entryway, into the heart of the central chamber and onto the back wall.

As the daylight receded, a slow entrancement placed me not quite in this world but rather slipping into another time, long ago. The feeling of home and longing only got stronger as we penetrated deeper into the mound. The thick air was alive and charged with ions; I saw stones with blue nimbuses at the edges as we passed into the central area.

Our guide suggested that bones had once been laid in the basins so the souls to whom they belonged would be released into the light for re-birth as the solar rays came to illuminate the inner sanctum. The guide illuminated the magnificent, high, corbelled roof as he spoke and then doused his torch so we could experience total, silent darkness of this sacred space. Thousands of years and as many souls who had lived and left here pressed in upon me. I began weeping, tears tracking silently down, my heart suspended in melancholy.

Out of the indigo gloom came the three sacred birds of the "summer triangle" star constellation: Cygnus the swan, Aquila the eagle, and Lyra the vulture. They guard the top of the northern skies in autumn and were considered the original sacred trinity who live in the abode of the immortals.

I had come here expecting nothing; I have no Irish blood. Yet a flood of memories returned as Cygnus held me close, flying as it does into the Great Rift of the Milky Way, the original road of death and rebirth for the ancients. I recalled long nights watching the stars, doing the slow, important work of knitting the living with the dead, the heavens with the earth, the Great Mother with her creations.

Our guide relit his torch, and we were free to roam the outer corridors, making our way out at our own pace. I spent some time sitting in one of the shorter arms, where walls lined with great tall stones were traced with spirals. Brooding over the basin there, I worked to put the torrent of vision and deep heart shining into some order.

Eventually, I staggered shakily down the dim main corridor. A small voice murmuring at the midway told me to touch the walls. My hand brushed over a magnificent chevron of bird forms carved deeply into the side of one rugged wall stone. A sweet sweep of benediction washed over my body, cleansing it. Clearly, I was told to bear witness to the living Spirit; a bond that my soul once again became with aligned over the coming days.

As we made our way up the coast to Northern Ireland, this alignment came in the form of impossibly close encounters with birds, the key, sacred totems of the ancient, great Goddess. Of course, there are always birds around everywhere, but these were of a certain kind and did not act like creatures minding their own business. After we exited the passageway at Brú na Bóinne, swaggering ravens appeared at every stop, laughing, and flaunting themselves when we paused to view scenery along the road.

While standing on a little bridge over a quiet pool, three white swans appeared out of a channel hidden in the thickets, gliding out and performing an elaborate waltz right in front of me, then swam silently away. As I walked on a pebbled beach, I suddenly found a smooth, chiseled, caramel-colored rock. It was not round like the rest and was marked in the middle with a perfect, white-crescent moon and star. Right then, a kestrel hovered to look into my eyes for a long moment; it took a bow neatly up and down before speeding away. Out on some high cliffs at an overlook, a golden eagle swooped to perch close on the remains of a field fence; he stood quietly long enough to make sure he was honored, feathers rustling in the wind.

I came at last to stand alone at the edge of rough sea breakers at the Giant's Causeway, singing a song of thanks to the spirits. A handsome grey heron alighted not four feet away, swaying in time to the lament, imprinting forever the timeless enfoldment in Spirit that was mine at Newgrange.

Marguerite Hafeman

HAVEN OF THE FAWNS

We arrived at the two-story vacation home in the mountains of Julian, California, the gentle scent of daffodils and bluebells floating in the air. There was no television here, only a radio playing light classical music. Every wall lined with shelves designed to adopt as many books as possible. Excitedly glancing at the titles, I wondered how many years it took to collect such timeless treasures. My heart smiled; I felt like I was in a "nirvana of knowledge."

As each day of our stay passed, a calm, magnetizing energy began to unveil itself. It exuded from the house, the land around it, and the big, black stones in clusters around the property. *Who flattened these stones, and why? It seems as if they weren't altered by nature.*

One day, when the property manager stopped by to water the plants, he found me resting on one of the stones, absorbing its vibration into my soul.

"Do you feel the energy in these stones?" he asked, smiling. "These are special rocks used long ago for Native American ceremonies. Their cores contain the wisdom and spirit of the land."

"Yes, I feel some kind of magnetism in them," I replied. Their energy left me with an enigmatic sense of completeness. It made me not want to go anywhere else.

Day after day, invisible layers of me peeled off. I could see myself with extra clarity and began bringing in new changes to heal my life.

I discovered an antique wooden box filled with letters written long ago by the home's original owners. The current homeowners had left these for visitors to enjoy. Pictures of those first owners hung on the walls, radiating a sense of their unseen presence. I began connecting to their souls via these images. Their wisdom floated to the back of my head, slowly and frequently. From their letters I learned that both were writers and contributing editors to multiple magazines.

During our stay I perceived a strong, inviting, and hospitable energy. On occasion I felt guided to read a particular book from the collection. The information I received from all those books was for my growth, expansion of my viewpoints, and so much more. Other times, I felt guided to look outside the kitchen window and observe the visits of the wild turkeys or the families of deer with their baby fawns who would drop by and peacefully graze. All these experiences left me with a tender and lasting joy.

Each day, various wild animals and the most beautiful birds would visit the land around the property. They were not at all afraid of witnessing our presence. They did what they came here to do: connect with the spirit of the property and the stones. They came to experience this zone of serenity.

Over the years, we visited this home multiple times to continue replenishing our souls, minds, and bodies. Other visitors took the time to share their experiences and wrote heartfelt reviews in an attractive notebook resting on an end table. They all, without exception, said they felt an internal healing, a recalibration of the self-energy field, and a thirst to return for more.

For me, this unique, magnetizing land opened a world of unity, unspoken love, and most of all, quietude. I became one with everything. I was blissful and serene, effortlessly soaking up the energy of bountiful love. Thus, I joined those enlightened by the spirit of the land and chose the path of a writer.

Ida Ra Nalbandian

THE BODY REMEMBERS

*I*t had been a long time since I had felt so much joy moving through my body. I had been surrounded by grief for years since my mother and father died.

Was it the colors in the paintings on the wall? The light streaming into the plaza? I couldn't tell what caused it, but a fantastic energy overcame me. I felt so happy and alive.

I belong here.

For the past three years, I had been moving through loss and sadness. I was questioning my purpose. *Who was I?*

My life felt full of heartbreaking emotions. My parents were now gone. My children were grown up and off building their lives. I had broken up with my partner. Even my clients were finishing their work with me and moving on.

I felt alone. I hoped a retreat would help me to recover and renew my spirit.

So here I was, standing in the *Palacio de Tepantitla* in Teotihuacan, a vast Mexican archaeological complex northeast of Mexico City. The site is full of Aztec, Mayan, and Toltec traditions.

Suddenly, I wasn't lonely. I was feeling joy, a deep knowing. It was both rejoicing and overwhelming. I felt alive again.

I overheard my teacher explain, "This was a temple where mystics were sent to learn and train."

The paintings on the wall expressed this period. Enchanted by the colors in the images, I turned to my teacher and asked, "The paintings were with pigments of the earth, right?"

"What do you think?" she said.

Hell yeah. You painted them, Terri. You lived here. You were a mystic who came to live and study here. You still carry this energy, is what I heard.

My hands tingled as if I'd been painting for days. There it was: a message from my soul, loud and clear. I had lived, studied, painted, loved, and laughed—all of it—right here. My whole being knew this. The passion was so alive.

My body remembered.

As I stood there with my eyes closed, I soaked up the light, the memories, the feelings of joy. Intoxicated, I wanted to stay forever.

Teo was a portal of energy for me. It was clear to me now that I had been one of the mystic souls chosen to live and learn these ancient teachings. I understood why I had seen orbs of colors as I walked through the different plazas. As I investigated more of the rooms and paintings, memories uplifted my heart. Joy enveloped me while we were in the *Plaza of Tepantitla*.

As we walked to the next site, my energy dropped and felt heavy again. My mind raced as I tried to figure out what had happened. *Stay out of the old story*, I kept telling myself. *Stay out of the mind.* But there it was again: the feelings of loss, death, grief, and separation.

When we stopped at a beautiful old red pepper tree, all I could do was cry. The tree was in bloom, and it called to me in remembrance. But I was overcome with sadness and tears. *Enough grief!* I kept thinking. *I've got to let this go.* But my sadness was being triggered again. Why?

The message came to me as I stood under the pepper tree. I knew I had died here, painting the walls, and learning the teachings of the mystery schools. The tree brought forth this memory. *I died too young.* That was the anguish I was feeling after we left Tepantitla. It wasn't grief for my mother or father but for this young mystic who had been so happy and alive—who had been me.

It seemed the grief of my soul had been triggered, and I couldn't tell one lifetime from another. I walked with this sadness, my tears flowing.

We arrived at the Palace of the Jaguars and entered the Palace Quetzalpapalotl, also known as the "Temple of the Butterflies." The light there was amazing. My eyes were wide open as the illumination moved through me. It was trying to help me heal. Yet I couldn't stop crying.

When we came out, my teacher saw that I was weeping and emotional as the memories flooded in at once. It was becoming too much to handle. She turned me around and told me to face the Pyramid of the Moon.

"Bring all the energy you feel into your womb. Embody the energy," she said.

I took a deep breath, held it in, and began to calm down. When I opened my eyes, I was staring right at the pyramid. Incredible blue light, the aura of the Pyramid of the Moon, shone around it. It was glowing and vivid, reminding me I could see light and auras. This blue light confirmed my gift of clairvoyance. My teacher told me again to take this knowledge into my womb.

The body remembers.

As I stood there breathing into my womb, I came back into my body with this wisdom. I understood why I had wanted to do this work, to understand my soul better. I was confirming my path, my purpose, in this lifetime. And I already had the knowledge, even if buried deep within.

Breathing with this awareness, I started to release my pain. In that moment of recognition, as I acknowledged all I had learned, I remembered the wisdom of these teachings. It was wisdom I could now tap into in my present life. Grief no longer riddled my body. I felt free.

My life continues with this remembrance of my soul. I have noticed a shift in my confidence and understanding of these gifts. My joy has returned.

Terri Ann Heiman

A DIRTY OLD ROCK

othing I had read or experienced on my vast travels prepared me for the strange feeling of knowing, awe, and comfort I experienced at the temple pyramids of Palenque, the jungle home of the Lacondon Maya.

Had I been here before?

Immediately enamored by these people and this place, I felt surrounded by mystery as I wandered and learned of the Temple of Inscriptions and the burial chamber and sarcophagus of the King, Pakal the Great. I was blown away by doors and windows in the shape of a capital T, indicating a sacred crossing into other dimensions and worlds, both without and within. I wandered through buildings and grassy expanses, feeling deep beauty and surreal, spiritual reverence for the small and large temples with their strange names and ancient architecture. I wanted something this place had to offer.

Palenque had been part of the Maya world. I knew of the work of the shaman priests, importance of their decisions, and the powerful wisdom they passed on to other Mayan states and temple priests. I learned of the jaguars and their role in guiding the people. The priests interpreted the shamanic dreams and visions and the messages sent via these dreams to inform and give guidance from the ancestors. I saw visions of the priests chanting wisdom into the temple rocks as I felt the power of the temple buildings.

I wandered past the allowed tourist area to where they were unearthing a new temple, rock by rock. I wanted a piece of it but felt I could not take anything from this sacred site. The ground was slippery, and I lost my footing. As I did so, I found a chip of the limestone from one of the temple rocks and profusely thanked who-knows-who.

Why was I so reverent? I didn't know, but I felt a strong connection to the ancient sacredness at the site.

Toward the end of the day, I was waiting for my friend near the temple entrance, where a Ceiba tree provided shade for me to sit under. Because I didn't know how long I would have to wait, I closed my eyes and began to meditate. Soon, I heard a *clop! clop!* and something landed at my feet. I discovered a fist-sized piece of limestone, whispered "Thank you!" and hid it in my pocket.

Wow! The rock had hit the tree twice before landing right at my feet, bypassing the many tourists wandering out of the temple grounds at close of day. *Where did it come from? How did they know I wanted a piece? Why did I want a piece? Why did they give it to me? Who are they? How did they throw it so accurately?* My mind raced.

Okay. The temples are magic, I know that. They clearly were used for sacred purposes. And the priests here shared knowledge with shaman priests from all over Mayan territory. *Ancestors may still guard the temples. Do I even believe all this?* I wondered.

Back at the hotel in San Cristobal de las Casas, I looked at the piece of limestone. It was nothing special—just a dirty rock with a triangular depression. It fit easily in the palm of my hand, but I didn't understand its use or significance. Could I reach the ancestors through this bit of stone?

My life changed completely that day. I asked the rock to teach me more about the Maya, and it delivered. I learned of the work of the shaman priests, the importance of their decisions, and the powerful wisdom they passed on to other Mayan states and temple priests. I learned of the jaguars and their role in guiding the people. The priests interpreted the shamanic dreams, visions, and the messages sent via these dreams to inform and give guidance from the ancestors.

As I learned of their love of crystals, I wanted crystal jewelry for the first time. Crystals connect me to Mayan kings and ancestors. I learned of other sacred sites in Peru, other lives I have led, and ceremonies I performed there. The rock gives me messages for people I have not yet met from countries I have never been. It informs me of things I must study and helps me hear Quetzalcoatl when he speaks to me.

The dirty old limestone rock from Palenque now sits on my altar in a place of deep respect as I continue to learn from the Maya.

Thea Hollett

THE RAINBOW RACE

The plane swerved a little as the wheels hit the tarmac. I grinned nervously. This was it—my new home in the Peruvian Andes. Since the first time I had visited Cuzco, twelve years earlier, I had known I would move here one day. Now the time had arrived.

After meeting my new landlord and depositing my bags in the unfamiliar room, I collapsed onto the bed. Altitude and jetlag combined to create a fuzzy feeling of deep exhaustion. I was just drifting onto the dream plane when I felt her call.

No, Pachamama, I can't. Not today. Let me come up there tomorrow.

As I rolled over and tucked the blankets up around my head, her pull intensified. The Great Mother was calling me to the powerful portal at the Temple of the Moon. It was only a forty-five-minute walk for someone acclimated to the altitude. In my state, it would easily take twice as long.

After dragging myself into a taxi to fetch fresh flowers from the market, I headed to the portal. The climb up felt like scaling Everest. The air was so thin, and my body had not yet adjusted. Every few meters, I needed to rest.

Tears sprung to my eyes as I stepped through the gateway. This was my soul place. I could feel the exact moment I left the city and entered the magical portal of this land. The sounds of cars faded, replaced with the gentle creaking of eucalyptus tree branches rubbing against each other. These tall guardians were welcoming me home.

After asking permission to enter the space and offering a single sunflower, I continued up the mountain. The air was crisp, and the sun had a strong bite. I stopped by the Temple of the Moon to catch my breath. The stunning view into the mountains and valleys never grew old for me. The babbling of the stream below filled the air as white and yellow butterflies danced together. From somewhere in the distance, the enchanting sound of a Peruvian flute wafted on the wind. I scanned the ridges but couldn't see the musician. They had found their own little sanctuary amongst the rocks and hills.

I crossed the brook and climbed the next hill. My legs felt weak as waves of emotion pulsed through me. The land opened to me, and the energy magnified. Finding a peaceful spot, I sat and pulled out my offerings. I kicked off my shoes and socks and plunged my toes into the grass. It was stiff and scratchy at the end of the dry season.

Collecting nearby rocks, I made a circle for my offering and drizzled Florida water around the perimeter to create the ceremonial space. The potent scent was like a nurturing hug from the grandmothers of this land. With no sense of time, I honored the land and offered the commitment of my highest service. There was no plan. I had no idea why I had been called back here or what I would be creating, but it didn't matter. I knew it would all unfold. For now, I announced my arrival and asked the land to receive and hold me.

After singing and playing my medicine drum, I expressed my gratitude by laying out an altar of fresh flowers and *mapacho*, sacred Peruvian tobacco. With eyes closed, I took a moment and held my hands over my heart. As I looked up to thank the great *Apu*, the mountain spirit, what I saw made my jaw drop. No more than ten meters before me hovered a pillar of rainbow light. It stood vertically, unlike any rainbow I had ever seen. And there was no rain in sight.

Overcome by it all, I sat perfectly still, afraid that moving or even breathing too deeply would break the magic. Then I heard her.

Go into the rainbow, she said.

I furrowed my brow. I was on a ridge and the rainbow was over the edge. There was no physical way to walk there.

Go into the rainbow.

Again, the words of Pachamama filled my heart. I unfocused my eyes and tuned into the energy of the rainbow. For a while nothing happened, and I grew frustrated that I wasn't getting it, whatever 'it' was.

Taking a few breaths to reset and let go of expectations, I tried again. As I eased more and more into stillness, I started to feel the frequency of the rainbow. The bands of color began to move. Or perhaps they had already been pulsating and I hadn't been able to see it. The violet expanded and became the whole pillar. Next the blue and magenta expanded and pulsated.

I gasped. Suddenly, I knew that the rainbow was communicating with me. It wasn't just colors—it was *consciousness*. The shock of the realization snapped me out of my connected state and soon the rainbow faded and disappeared.

That night, as I lay in bed, all I could think about was the connection I had felt with the rainbow. It had been consciousness. But what had it been trying to tell me? There was a deep stirring within me. I knew that something enormous had happened.

The next day, I went to the area where I could catch a local bus. Each bus had a unique name, so I asked a police officer which bus would take me to Real Plaza.

"*Arcoiris*," he responded.

I stared at him, dumbfounded. *Arcoiris* meant "rainbow" in Spanish. He pointed to the corner as a white bus with a rainbow painted on the front approached.

A year and a half passed. I was guided to different power places: Egypt, Spain, and Mexico. Each time codes and messages were shared with me. Rainbows kept coming into my experience in different ways, yet I still had no idea why.

One day, I went to my friend's house opposite the Temple of the Moon. As I rested on the grass in her beautiful garden, I could feel the energetic pulse of this powerful portal. I closed my eyes. Suddenly, cosmic images swirled in my third eye and I sensed a powerful presence: the Great Cosmic Mother. The intensity filled me with fear. I felt myself being forced to expand, as though I were being pulled apart. It was too much! I snapped my eyes open and tried to shake off the connection, but she didn't leave. She was inside me and all around me.

I'm not ready, I begged.

Yet the more I resisted, the more overwhelming her energy became. How was there so much? Why wouldn't it stop? I knew the power of the land I was on, but this was on a whole other level. Even as the fear pounded within my chest and belly, I knew I had to allow it. Digging deep, I breathed out and closed my eyes once more.

Okay, Great Mother. What is it?

A huge swell of energy enveloped me. I felt like I became the cosmos. Stars and comets and bright colors danced around me. They *were* me. I was everything at once. It reminded me of how I had felt as a child. Then she spoke.

I will not be made small! I will not be put aside! I am the Divine Mother. I am within you. And when you fear me, you fear yourself. To come into your power, you must embody all that I am.

My back arched and I gasped as her force entered my heart. Creation was flooding my body, surging into every cell. I felt unlimited love, compassion, and strength as if I were the fabric of the cosmos itself. Feelings of unworthiness were forced from my body. There was no more resistance, nowhere to hide. She was everything and she was within me.

An hour passed. I didn't know. We were outside of time. But eventually, my breathing settled into a slow, deep rhythm. I felt a new soft and grounding energy, which I recognized instantly as the Divine Father. His energy was calm and stable. I felt him form a loving container around the vastness that was the Divine Mother within me. The two intertwined and came into one. It brought a sense of peace greater than I had ever known. The land around me fell into a reverent hush. The birds were quiet. Even the prickles seemed to adjust themselves to leave me be.

After a while, with my eyes still closed, I found myself in a beautiful place of pure white light. My heart was open, I could feel the light was love itself. Iridescent rainbow frequencies moved through the light, and I wondered where I was. The love was blissful. Never had I felt so complete. It wasn't about feeling like "me." It was far beyond that. I *was* love. I was whole. I was everything.

My mind kicked in for a moment, and I asked the question, *Why am I here?*

Within the pure white light, the rainbow frequencies started to form the shapes of beings. I looked on, amazed, having thought I had been alone on this wondrous plane. As the rainbows continued to move, a row of pure light beings appeared before me.

We are the Rainbow Race. And we have much to teach you. It's time for you to restore The Rainbow Tablets.

I shook my head in awe. I had no idea what the Rainbow Tablets were. Yet, at the core of my soul, I felt a deep sense of remembering. The Rainbow

Race stood before me. Whatever the Rainbow Tablets were, I couldn't wait to find out.

Sia-Lanu Estrella

UPON THE GLASTONBURY TOR

Tales of Celtic lore have always fascinated me. The settings for ancient adventures and adventurers left me in awe as I heard the tales of Morgaine of the Fae in Avalon; her half-brother Arthur, who became the "Once and Future King;" Guinevere, his queen; and gallant Lancelot, who was both a sworn knight to Arthur and a champion for his queen.

Imagine my joy when a friend who had been to England many times invited me to join her upcoming trip to the merry old sod. She proposed an itinerary that set my heart all a-flutter with visits to such mystical places as Avebury, Stonehenge, and Glastonbury. My arrival in England on May Day hinted that magick was in the air, and I knew my passion for Celtic mystery would not be disappointed.

Our first stop was in glorious Glastonbury, home now to many people like me who prefer to live at a pace not as hectic as our modern times require. The gentler, calmer nature of the quaint village town was like stepping into a movie scene. This setting allowed me to drop my usual persona and feel my way into the story of a time I had experienced long ago. At least in my dreams...

After checking in to our charming bed and breakfast, my friend met some acquaintances, and I was free to roam around. I visited the ancient Glastonbury Cathedral ruins, the underground White Spring from which the sacred male energies of the region came forth, and the ever-so-serene Chalice Well, from which the sacred feminine energies arise from deep within Mother Earth and has been a site of recorded healings for more than a thousand years.

As I approached the land formation known as the Tor, I could feel the energies moving, dancing, and playing in a way I'd never experienced before. As the sun started to set, I was awash in anticipation that the magickal mystery tour I desired was quite possible. I approached the base of the Tor and bowed my head in prayer, asking for insight and guidance for my life.

Ascending the spiraling paths created by centuries of pilgrims' feet connecting to the same magnetism I was now experiencing lifted my consciousness beyond my personality and welcomed me to an energy beyond space and time. At one point in my climb, I needed to sit and take in the view. Squatting on the side of this mini mountain, I communed with the local rabbits and sheep grazing there before continuing to the ruins of the church tower called St. Michael's, which crowns the earthly temple.

It was now dusk, and the air was like a plasma field. As I finally reached the top, I felt my gaze directed to a spot hundreds of yards away. I realized I was not alone. Some shadowy figure stood inside the tower in a pensive or reflective manner, arms crossed and head bowed.

I felt the need to let him be alone for a few more minutes before I moved into that space. I asked my guidance if I should be troubled by this presence and was informed, *No need.* Suddenly, the person inside the tower picked up their head and looked directly at me across the distance. He appeared to be male. When our eyes met, I saw with other than my 3-D eyes. My consciousness had met with his.

He asked telepathically, *Can you see me?*

I answered, *Yes.*

He abruptly left the wall he had been leaning upon and headed toward the tower exit at the point farthest from me. As he walked away, I moved closer. Just before he reached the exit, he turned to look at me again. I was aware that he was assessing me. He surprised me when, instead of leaving through the open doorway at the end of the building, he turned to face one of the immensely thick stone walls of the church—and walked right through it.

I ran to the tower to look for him. *He must be visible; he was right here just a second ago!* As I peered around a corner, I spotted him in the growing darkness. He was already halfway down the Tor and heading toward a stand of trees. I followed.

He stopped again in front of the trees and turned to face me. As he did this, he grew in stature. His form expanded to almost Hulk-like proportions, and he addressed me again.

You cannot come with me.

This statement confirmed he was reading my thoughts. I was ready to leave this mortal coil and experience the realms of magick and mystery that had filled my heart for as long as I could remember.

Again, he said, *You cannot come with me*, and he dissolved into thin air.

Sitting in stunned wonder, I received this message: *Gwynn ap Nudd has honored you with his presence and attention. Go now in peace and keep your human heart open. Share your open heart with your world. It is very much in need of open hearts. Be brave.*

Kathleen Dale

THE DAY I DISAPPEARED

t was a gorgeous early morning with a clear blue sky. The sea sparkled in the sunshine, waves gently shushing on the shore. Even the trees welcomed the day, leaning into the light as I took my daily walk around the edge of a national park.

The trail began as a narrow track, more like a goat track, and I watched where I put my feet in case any little stone or root might choose to trip me up. Coming up to a patch of low, scrubby, paper bark trees the track changed, becoming cool and a little dark.

I actively avoid low and dark places because they feel oppressive in a vaguely threatening kind of way. If I can, I choose the high road, one bathed in light. But there was no avoiding this area. It was a few hundred steps, and I picked up speed as I walked, anxious to be out of the gloom.

Suddenly, a flash of vivid blue streaked in front of me so fast and close that I felt the brush of air on my skin. I stopped dead, my heart racing. He stopped, too. It was a blue wren, just an arm's length from me. Landing on a low branch, he hopped to face me and looked straight into my eyes. As he began to chatter vociferously, I was mesmerized. I didn't understand what he was saying, but whatever it was, he demanded my full attention.

I had no sense that I had intruded in any way. The bird was not aggressive, just insistent. Then he stopped. During a moment of complete silence, we contemplated each other. Then he flew off, back the way he had come, without ceremony or fuss. But I was left with the distinct impression that he was saying to himself, *Job done.*

The mystery to me was, *What job?* I had never seen a blue wren in this part of the country. *Why now? Why here?*

His chattering came back to me when I reached where the track ran along a cliff top. This part of the walk always scared me. My legs became weak, my heart pounded, and most terrifying of all, I felt an almost overwhelming compulsion to succumb to the beckoning of the deep, pulsing water below, to approach that dangerous crumbling cliff edge and fall into ghastly oblivion.

Was the bird's message a warning?

Every morning I braced myself to pass this section. I asked myself why I thought I needed to put myself through this terror time and time again.

It never helped that my logical mind said, *You are creating a reality that doesn't exist.* The pull felt real. It was powerful and visceral—not a figment of my imagination.

But this morning, a voice said as strong as that little bird had spoken to me, *Look at the sky, look at the track. There are other people up ahead in the distance. It is safe. You are not going to fall.*

I stopped and took a huge breath. The urge to run away still clung to me. My body was at once shaking and leaden. Slowly, I put one foot in front of the other, until I could no longer feel that appalling pull over the cliff's edge. Trembling with my clothes drenched with sweat, I sank to the ground, thankful to feel its stony solidity beneath me.

Everything was easy after that. Strolling along, even on the steeper bits of the track, enjoying the smell of the bush and the ocean, feeling the warmth of the sunshine on my face, came as sheer relief. I was unconcerned by the residual quivering in my stomach.

Suddenly, I disappeared. Quite literally, I disappeared.

There was no me. I had no body, not even a sense of physical presence. I felt that if somebody touched me, their hand would go straight through me, like how people's hands go through ghosts in the movies.

I wasn't *frightened*. "Awe-struck" best describes it. Nothing in my life had ever felt like this. *How could my body disappear?* One moment it was there, and the next, it had blipped out. Oddly, it felt wonderful—light, spacious, and yet subtly, contained. It was the lightness that I really loved. No weight to carry around.

However, in some mysterious way, at some level, I was still walking. The scenery was changing, and I sensed something happening at ground level, some movement—but it didn't seem to belong to me. I floated up the hill with no sense of the effects of gravity. At the top, I stopped and looked out over the ocean. Everything was the same but a bit brighter.

Kerry the human had no material presence, no felt sense of a body. I was also aware that I was aware, and I could consciously switch between the two perspectives.

Then, as suddenly as it had come, the feeling left. My body became solid again. I sensed its weight. I could feel my breathing and the friction of clothes against my skin. I was visible again. The magical experience was over—but curiously, I experienced no sense of loss, just an "Oh!" of wonder.

I had survived the dangerous part of my hike and subsequent disappearance. I was back in my body, back on the trail, and it was still a beautiful morning. Everything was normal again.

Except that I was forever changed.

Kerry Lyons

SACRED FIRE OF PASSAGE

ime stands still as I sit, enshrouded in a thick cloak of sorrow and pain. Not even an hour earlier, my younger sister had called with the devastating news of the passing on of my dear older brother. She had planned to visit him in the hospital the following day, and I had asked her to pass my love to him through the dense veil of his comatose state. I believed that he could hear us.

My soul cries out to the Divine, to the universe, and to God—not asking for answers, but in deep pain and anguish as I realize that my brother, as I knew him, is no longer on this earthly plane. Love, sorrow, suffering, regret, separation—a scenic montage of many memories, are compressed into this moment and squeezes my heart with indescribable emotions. My cry a deep lament, a profound prayer that only my soul knows, and Divine Spirit can hear.

I long to be with my sisters and my mum, but I am too far away. My mortal weakness and humanness know no other outlet except to feel what I'm feeling, and I surrender to that. In this divinely ordained time, I'm sitting outside an Om chanting circle, ready to open my wounded heart to the infinite portal that the sacred chants will create on this auspicious twelfth day of the twelfth month.

I'm not chanting. I cannot chant with my constricted throat and flowing tears. I cannot sit in a circle with the others, so I sit as far away as I can to create a filtering boundary between my despair and the chanting. In my muted silence and with my eyes closed, I let the beautiful sounds and gentle rhythm of the room wash over me in soothing waves that help calm my anguished spirit.

My awareness of the circle before me is fading, and I am drifting slowly away, though I can still hear the soporific Om chants. I see another circle as I stand in a dim, open plain, my spirit guide beside me, his arm around my shoulder. Forest surrounds us; silhouettes of great trees stand still and imperious, framing a clearing in which burns a huge fire. Around that hypnotic fire, many of my ancestors who have passed on are seated.

My heart lurches as I see my dad. He is looking solemn, almost stoical. I am reminded of his countenance during holy celebrations at home. My paternal grandparents, aunt, and others sit in the circle with him. These were people who had shared special bonds with my brother.

They all have thick blankets around their shoulders and are gazing pensively into the fire. I wonder if they can also hear the chants. *How is that possible?* I wonder.

I want to run forward and embrace my father tightly, even if just for a moment, but my spirit guide's hand on my shoulder and a deep inner knowing restrains me. Instead, I keep vigil in awe and reverent wonder. It is a hauntingly beautiful and power-filled, sacred sight. I can almost feel the warmth of the roaring fire whose dancing flames cast illuminating shadows on their faces.

My dad looks up and to the other side. My heart stops beating! I see a figure approaching from the shadows. Even before his form is illuminated by the glow of the golden firelight, I know it's my brother. He treads slowly, yet surely, deliberately. He looks healed and whole, the young, handsome man he was before life's hand robbed him of his fair portion. My father slowly, yet purposefully rises and goes to him with outstretched arms that speak eloquently in the poignant, gentle silence. Dad lovingly wraps a blanket around my brother's shoulders and escorts him to the circle around the fire.

My brother and father sit next to each other. Everyone is quiet, as they have been all along, but now I sense a joyous peace in them; they have serene smiles. A feeling of completeness permeates the luminescent scene. The fire seems bigger and brighter, and I feel a fire burning within me. I am ablaze with love and emotions.

As the rich, wondrous tones of the Om chants sound in the distance, my father gets up, gently touching my brother and motioning to him to do the same. They stand in a clearing closer to the fire. Everyone else begins to rise, and they encircle my brother, stretching their arms and blankets around him, forming a screen. The scene unfolds in slow-motion surrealism before me, in dense, muted, marbled colors of grey, green, black, and bits of orange, red, and amber. My brother is now totally obscured from view as the veil of thick, intertwined blankets rise like great wings around him. As I watch in fixated enthrallment, this silent circle of forms, ethereal in the firelight, begins to fade, getting dimmer and dimmer.

I want to scream out, "No! Please stay!"

My throat feels choked, a hard lump resting where my voice should be. Where they had been standing moments ago, now only a wisp of smoke remains. Then that, too, evaporates into nothingness.

The crisp tinkle of a bell signals the end of the Om chanting, gently piercing my reverie. Back in the room, I feel utterly strange and bereft of words. I am in this world, yet not of this world, as I float between realms, unsure if the veils are drawn apart or closed. Yet I also feel a deep calm, permeating peace, and gratitude for what I have just witnessed.

Travel well, my dear brother, ensconced in the warm, protective light and love of our elders leading the way. I know not the path you now travel, yet I know my heart has created space to hold your memory in eternity, as it had done so many years ago when Dad had begun his journey across the bridge of timelessness. I feel my healing has begun…

Cyndae Cerridwyn Stephens

JERUSALEM, THE LIGHT, AND ME

*T*he *Via Dolorosa*—also known as "The Way of the Cross"—was the site of Jesus's final journey through the streets of Jerusalem as he carried his cross to where he was crucified. The Church of the Holy Sepulcher now stands on that spot.

I had the honor of visiting that spot years ago when I was a trainer with the Anti-Defamation League and selected with thirty-nine other educators nationwide to participate in a ten-day scholarly program to study the Holocaust and how to teach it at Yad Vashem, the World Holocaust Remembrance Center.

We spent our days in Jerusalem in intensive study, both in formal classes and touring the monuments, memorials, and museums at Yad Vashem in addition to evening events and tours of the Old City. After our last day of classes, we were granted a special tour of the Church of the Holy Sepulcher.

The church a massive stone structure that has seen centuries of destruction and repair. It is a metaphor for survival, and its large wooden front doors are a weighty invitation to its sacred history.

The first place we experienced was the Altar of the Crucifixion. Underneath the altar was an opening in the floor that revealed the stone where Christ's cross had stood. We saw many visitors ahead of us kneeling and reaching under the altar to touch the stone. Our group followed suit.

We were then led to another large room to see the Stone of Anointing. It commemorates the place where Jesus's body was prepared for burial. From there we entered the Rotunda, a voluminous, round space with a dome ceiling. A hole in the center of the ceiling is surrounded by a burst of decorative golden rays, and arched windows encircle the dome's perimeter. In the center of the room is the Edicule, a small stone structure enclosing the sepulcher where it is believed Jesus had been entombed.

The rays of the late afternoon sun streaming through one of the arched windows formed a circle on the floor like a spotlight. Sunbeams danced like snowflakes caught in this light shaft. It was the perfect invitation for a photo op, and many tourists were taking advantage of it.

One of our group members, Bill, had become our official trip photographer. Bill thought this illuminated circle would be a great place for our group to take photos too. As each of us stepped into the light, we reacted differently. Some hammed it up, striking a dramatic or comical pose. Some tried to look up at the light but immediately squinted and either turned away or shielded their eyes because it was so bright. I was last in line, and as I stepped into the spotlight, I felt compelled to kneel. I knelt on my right knee and looked up toward the light.

"Move forward just a little," Bill said. "You're in the shadow."

As I leaned forward and lifted my head, my gaze was met by the most magnificent, gorgeous white light. I was compelled to raise my left hand to it, and I looked right into its glory. I did not need to squint, and I was not blinded. I just kept gazing at it, mesmerized. And in that instant—it took me!

For a moment that felt like eternity, I was no longer *me*. I felt only joy, peace, and love as if I were giving and receiving love simultaneously. I felt unconditional love and at the same time, I loved everything and everyone.

However, the quality of that love was unlike anything I had ever experienced. It was bigger, certain, and complete.

In that moment, I was everyone and everything in the past, present, and future—but there was no distinction between those periods. It was all now. I was detached from all things physical, including my body. Yet I had a fine, sharp sense of total clarity that I was part of the All.

Looking into the glory of that white light, I felt and knew with such keen certainty that I was home. In that state, I was complete. I needed nothing. I wanted nothing except to stay there forever.

"Oh wow!" was all I could say at that moment.

"My God, Alisa, you look like an angel!" Bill said as he took my picture.

I do not know how long I was in that space. It felt like time had stopped. I had become a resonant being, and I was home.

Then suddenly, as if someone had snapped their fingers, it was over. It felt as if I were awakening from a hypnotic trance or the moment in Cinderella when the clock struck midnight. There I was, dropped back down onto the cold marble floor completely transformed, and resonating with the gift of this experience with Divine Light.

I moved through the rest of the tour as if I were in a dream. As detached as I felt from everything, I also seemed connected to everyone and everything. I was filled with this deep love and sense of peace, certain about what I had just experienced, even though I didn't know what to do with it or what it meant for my future. I knew I was not the same me who had boarded the plane ten days earlier, and I had not been given this gift randomly or arbitrarily.

I felt expanded. I was not only feeling the love of the Light, I *was* the love of the Light.

Alisa M. Parcells

SEEKING THE ORACLE

*T*ime took on greater meaning here.

The ancient, mythic ritual sites of Mycenae, the Sanctuary of Asklepios at Epidaurus, the Minoan palace at Knossos, and the awe-inspiring Temple of Apollo at Delphi were breathtaking reminders of what it takes to build and create something of infinite beauty and wonder— forever imbued within these sacred sites.

Captivated by the mystery of these portals of transformation, I tried to imagine the people who had created these astounding monuments and the massive efforts required to build them. I believe it was for the higher purpose of uniting earthly humans with the gods. These mysteries remain, as does the power that emanates from these revered thresholds.

Before seeking the counsel of the great oracle at the Temple of Apollo at Delphi, I prepared myself, as was the tradition. I cleansed my face in the Castalian Spring and drank the water before climbing the stone steps leading up to the temple. With great honor and reverence, I approached the sacred entrance where "Know Thyself" had been inscribed above the columns. Taking a deep breath to ground myself, I held my hands out to receive.

Bravely I asked, "What is the greater purpose in writing about my journey to Afghanistan in 1977 and sharing the photographs I took before these ensuing decades of conflict?"

Within moments, a great tremble shook me and ran down my spine as it transported me back a thousand years. As I carefully opened my eyes, I saw a circle of goddesses surrounding and protecting me, with the Goddess Gaia in the center. The beauty was almost blinding.

You've been here before. You know the answers. Follow the dream, a resounding inner voice echoed from within me.

You have been graced with the higher purpose of being a witness, a thread-bearer, and an emissary of light to bring the hidden gems of this culture forward so the world can see the heart of the Afghan people. You were sent there to be present, to inspire a deeper understanding of their humanity, and humanize perceptions of all cultures. You were chosen to show life there during a time of great peace. This will never be seen or understood without your story and your photographs. Let it be so.

With a new sense of courage and understanding, I began to slowly awaken from my reverie. Standing in current time with the echoes of my sojourn still resonating, ancient and present time gently merged into one. Gaia and my protective circle of goddesses were now within me, ever available for my deepest inquiry or when I needed them for strength and grounding. They are my sacred link to Delphi.

Tears flowed down my face as I began to grasp the magnitude of my connection with the ancients and the profound assignment I had been given so long ago in a prophetic dream that would not cease until I listened:

Towering snowcapped mountains, stretching as far as the eye could see, rise high in the distance to touch the sky. Herds of magnificent horses thundered across vast plains, claiming their freedom. Colorful nomads in ornately embellished chapans wander in long columns as they lead their camels across the rugged landscape. Haunting musical refrains begin to play amidst this exotic terrain, with a tabla and tambour pulsating a rhythmic beat. Everything reached into me, becoming a part of me. Something profound was emerging. I was being called from afar—from where, I knew not.

Within a week after my profound dream, an opportunity had landed in front of me that I said *yes* to, not knowing its greater purpose. With camera in hand and trust in the universe, I had packed away my wonderful, creative life, said goodbye to friends, and headed 6,737 miles to Afghanistan, into the unknown.

Upon arriving home from Delphi, I sequestered myself for months while I wrote and rewrote about my journeys. I poured myself into them, along with the messages from the oracle that helped me dream them into being. My photographs and writing are my "Gifts of History." I share them with open hearts everywhere that appreciate the value of every culture.

Now imbued with new insights from the Oracle at Delphi, I understand that we don't always see why we are called somewhere. I am grateful for the oracle's guidance and my trust in the universe. I realize she had me in her arms all along.

Joanne Warfield

A CIRCLE OF EUCALYPTUS TREES

he sacred hills surrounding the old city of Jerusalem are a place of many portals—powerful locations connecting heaven and Earth. Places where people have built temples and created altars and saints from all religions experienced a revelation or found their last rest.

Scattered throughout the hills and valleys, between the Dead Sea to the east and the Mediterranean Sea to the west, are also numerous hidden temporary portals that offer a door to additional realities and the unity of our essence and humanity.

On a sunny winter morning, I met with a group of friends for a ceremony of gratitude. Our plan was to gather at one of the many forests between the villages in which we lived, just down the slopes from the city of Jerusalem.

As we walked into the forest the smell of fresh earth filled our lungs. The ground was wet from earlier rain, but now the sun was shining, creating a perfect winter day to be outside. We thought we knew where we were headed until we heard the whisper of leaves—an invitation reaching through the roots and soil.

Two of us stopped to listen, breathing the invitation in and agreeing to leave the beaten path. Not far away was a circle of eucalyptus trees that bent inward. Their treetops formed a high dome, fully symmetrical, open to the sky above.

Some of us felt the veil, a thick yet flowing curtain of energy that stretched deep down into the earth around the trees and continued upwards to the few clouds scattered in the sky above us.

As part of our ritual, we each picked up something from the natural world around us and placed it in the center of our human circle: an offering that formed a wordless connection to the surrounding beauty. On our way, one member picked up a wounded butterfly. She placed it under the sun's rays.

The energy of the portal was powerful. With no effort, density was released. With grace, we embraced luminosity and shed tears. We exchanged hugs as we received a gift reminding us of who we each are. Standing within the portal and being embraced by an energetic healing frequency that leaves no room for confusion—we remembered. Each of us felt love, clarity, and togetherness.

As we returned to local time and grounded back to our physical reality, most of us found it difficult to leave. We sat within this sacred circle of trees, a portal of healing, for as long as our hearts guided us. We decided to leave our offerings in the center as they were and let the energy simmer. I was to come back the following day and return the space to the way it was before our presence.

The following day, I woke up expanded. As soon as I had a moment to myself, I sat with my journal and tried to put the previous day's experience into words: the powerful energy, the sense of flow, the ease and grace in which healing and clarity came through, and the comfortable silence between us. We had been held by the portal's energy, individually and as one. We each had gone through what we needed to, and at the same time, we healed something collectively for ourselves, our group, our children, and the earth we walk on.

We had been gifted with a moment, a simple, aligned intention of gratitude met by the universe. Only when I had brought some clarity to the experience did I fulfill my promise and return to the circle of eucalyptus trees.

As I reached the site, the trees welcomed me as they never had before and haven't done so since. The rocks, the twigs, and some of the leaves placed the day before were all there, but the butterfly was not.

Wishing for more nourishing energies from the day before, I sat to meditate, connecting to the earth below and the opening in the tree dome above. When I opened my eyes, numerous butterflies danced around me. It took my breath away.

Was the wounded butterfly among them? Was the butterfly healed now, along with our healing, expansion, and gratitude? My heart knows it was.

Efrat Shokef, Ph.D.

THE DOOR TO THE CRYSTAL CITY

*M*y flow of inspiration comes from natural Druidry. Intuitively I turn to the Earth, attracted to something deep underground. Exploring this realm has become one of my greatest passions, and this summer, was led to visit Mount Shasta, legendary for its portals leading to a vast, underground crystal city.

When the magnificent mountain—covered with shining, white snow even in the middle of a hot Californian summer—appeared in the distance, I started crying. My strong reaction surprised me. I sensed this visit was a homecoming, as if the mountain recognized me and I recognized him.

Everything shifted. I canceled my previously arranged accommodation and went camping in the wild to be as close to the mountain as possible. It had been a hot week in the town, and the deep forest felt more inviting.

The following days were full of adventurous exploration and peaceful connections with the many layers of this special place. The pinnacle of my trip came on the last day of my stay when I met an extraordinary man who became my guide. This charismatic gentleman, who appears suspiciously much younger than his age, was said to have physically visited the legendary crystal city of Telos—the city located beneath the mountain.

He told me that, a few years earlier, a portal had opened for him high up in the woods. He had emerged with the most fantastic descriptions of this Inner Earth kingdom, which is said to be inhabited by advanced beings who originally came from Lemuria. Beautiful, blond-haired human beings, much taller than we are, reside in this dazzling city all made of crystal, he said.

My new guide walked before me on a narrow footpath beside the sparkling McCloud Falls. At some point, I sensed an energy shift in the environment, as if we were crossing a barrier, getting closer to a place of power. When we passed a massive rock wall on the left, he suddenly stopped, turned around, and stretched his palm before my face.

"Stop here and turn left," he commanded, sounding like an otherworldly guardian.

My heart started beating stronger and my sight blurred as I followed his instructions. I found myself before a rock door. It was a perfect, human-sized door as if purposefully cut into the rock wall. Most tourists passed by without noticing. Apparently, noticing it was the first step of the activation.

As soon as I spotted the door, its magnetic attraction made me move closer. My whole body vibrated with this unknown energy that seemed to react to my presence. It drew me in as I took slow steps toward the door.

When I touched the central area of the door, I saw golden light patterns emerging from the stone: an eight-pointed star, a six-pointed star, and other geometrical symbols merged into each other. Together, they seemed like a flat image—but I saw they were multidimensional, expandable into space, so I could focus on them individually. Whichever one I focused on became more visible than the others.

On a rational level, I had no idea what the symbols meant, but I felt it was enough to observe them. On a deeper level, I somehow understood.

The golden light of the symbols got weaker when I stepped away from the portal. I tried to experiment with distances. At about 1.5 meters away, my sight became blurred. I had to be about one meter away to see the symbols.

I examined the surroundings of the portal and when I felt ready to leave, I decided to take a photo in front of the door. I set the camera and stood next to my guide. Suddenly, a strange stroke of energy hit me, and I lost consciousness for a couple of seconds.

I was used to the elevated energies of powerful places, but this one really shook me. I grabbed my stuff and made it a few meters further into a little clearing. I found a spot out of sight, behind a group of bushes, and laid down with my chest against the earth. My body was pulsating, my mind was empty, and I could feel myself breathing. It took several minutes, but Mother Earth helped me to integrate this experience, as she always does.

Deep within myself, I felt I had undergone a profound upgrade that would take its time to completely manifest. I embraced it with full trust, ready to reshape my life in whatever way was needed.

Michaela Dauriel

A TEAR IN THE FABRIC OF TIME

Stepping onto the ancient stones of Machu Picchu, I feel the sensation of being watched, of unseen eyes following my every move. It is an uncanny feeling that defies logic and reason yet courses through me with eerie familiarity. It is as though the spirits of this sacred place are walking beside me, whispering their secrets into my soul.

The physical challenges of the journey, including the steep ascent through the Andes that has made my limbs weary, all fade into insignificance in the face of the profound certainty that I have walked these paths before. I have stood in this very spot in another lifetime. It is as if time itself has folded back on me, and I am a traveler not just in space but in the realms of history and memory.

I take a moment to breathe the thin mountain air and take in the view. The towering peaks of the Andes stand sentinel, their ancient, weathered faces bearing witness to countless generations of humanity. The sky above is an impossibly deep shade of blue, a canvas for the cotton clouds that drift by. The sheer magnitude of this place and the awe-inspiring beauty of nature humble me to my core.

While my eyes are closed, a surge of energy, a spiraling vortex, emanates from the heart of Machu Picchu. It surrounds me, moving in a clockwise whirl, reverberating in all directions. It is as if the spirits of this place are inviting me to join in their cosmic dance, to become one with the pulsating heartbeat of the Earth. And in that moment, I see it: two colossal energy pyramids, one reaching up toward the heavens, the other plunging deep into the Earth. They feel like ancient guardians, keepers of wisdom and time. I am at their intersection, a humble witness to their power.

As I open my eyes once more, the world around me transforms. The mountains, which were once silent sentinels, now come alive as witnesses etched with stories. Geometric symbols and mesmerizing, intricate codes seem to materialize before me. They speak of a civilization that understood the language of the Earth, a people who communed with the spirits of the land.

Each stone, each ridge, each crevice tells a tale—a narrative woven into the fabric of this sacred place. A gnarled tree stands before me, its roots intertwined with ancient stones; I place my hand upon its rough bark and feel the heartbeat of the Earth beneath my fingertips. This tree has seen the centuries come and go and stood witness to the rise and fall of civilizations. Now, it shares its wisdom with me.

Wandering through the citadel—guided not by a map but by an inner knowing—every step, each stone I touch, is a communion with history and spirit. The air is imbued with palpable energy as if the molecules vibrate with a timeless resonance. This is a living library.

The clouds above shift and change, casting dappled shadows over the terraced fields below. In those fleeting moments of shadow and light, I see the ebb and eternal flow of life, the dance of creation and destruction. I understand that Machu Picchu is not just a monument to the past rather a living testament to the cycles of existence.

The day passes in a blur, yet each moment etched into my memory with exquisite clarity. The sun rises and sets over the ruins, painting the ancient stones with hues of gold and crimson. I sit in meditation, my gaze fixed on the horizon, and in those quiet moments, I feel a deep sense of peace and infinite expansion in my profound connection to the universe.

And then, as all journeys must, mine comes to an end. I descend from Machu Picchu, my heart brimming with gratitude. The physical world asserts itself once more, but I carry with me the knowledge that the magic of this place lives on, not just in the stones and the stories, but within me.

It is a tear in the fabric of time, a glimpse into the eternal, a testament to the enduring power of the human spirit to seek, discover, and to be transformed.

Hellevi E. Woodman

CHAPEL OF BONES

*T*he scream wormed its way up into my throat as I tried to sit quietly in the 15th-century Sao Francisco Church in Evora, Portugal. The large, Gothic-style church, built between 1475 and the 1550s, is one of a kind, thanks to its mesmerizing but macabre Chapel of Bones.

The carefully arranged skulls and bones of about 5,000 people cover the walls and columns within. My curiosity turned to concern as my small group approached the church, and I couldn't avoid the anxiety that began to grip me.

Heart fluttering, I approached this unusual religious structure. The rising feeling of alarm continued to niggle its way up through my body, along with chills, as I followed our tour guide, Joao, through the church to the famed Chapel of Bones.

As the group veered off to see this curiosity, I felt an intense need to sit down. My tears came, unbidden, as I connected to the souls within the space.

Red flames lashed the opening I had become, and I felt a rush of energy from my feet to the top of my head. Tears poured from my eyes as I struggled to stay still and silent.

I affirmed my commitment. *Just let it be. Be still. Be silent. Honor the process,* my inner voice spoke.

Embarrassed by my extreme reaction to what was otherwise a solemn atmosphere, I wondered: *Why isn't anyone else feeling this way? Why are they all curious and happy to view 5,000 bones of the poor and indigent, buried first in a small chapel graveyard—only to be dug up and used to decorate an adjunct enclosure to a church?*

My resentment was talking. I hadn't wanted to see this curiosity when I learned what it was. I had thought I would encounter holy relics and experience the profound energy to which I had become accustomed as I toured the megaliths, monoliths, Templar churches, and holy stone structures of Portugal.

But no, I had been pulled by some unforeseen force. It felt like a prison break. *Just my luck. Holy Hannah—would this never end?*

The rush of energy kept coming. My potent imagination saw a myriad of souls swimming toward the light through the portal that was my body.

Had they seen me coming? Was there a plan in place? Had I been lured there as an innocent bystander who had lost her way and stumbled into a trap? The spirit of inquiry kicked in as I detached from the visceral contact I felt.

Then, for a moment, I had a fleeting break. *Thank Goddess!*

Backstepping out of the experience and gaining an eagle view of the situation I found myself in, the dust settled into a clearer vision of my purpose.

Had I agreed to be present for this experience?

Something reminded me to view the present circumstances as a gift, not a trap. I believe there are no accidents or coincidences in life.

I gained equilibrium as the minutes passed. My tears subsided, and my anxiety diminished as my clarity grew. The temperature turned down. The fierce rush became more of a waterfall. I still had many questions, but I felt a deep sense of gratitude accompanied by feelings of calm and strength. Relief was in sight.

My dear friends surrounded me with hugs and words of encouragement. As soothed as my body felt, my mind and heart canvassed the myriad explanations for my unspoken question: *What just happened?*

Perhaps I had latched onto the holy location to release my own fears, negativity, and patterns that no longer served me. Maybe it had nothing to do with the bones and the chapel. I remained open to the idea that I chose this moment to liberate a pattern or paradigm of my own to the environment, to provide a home for what had been disrespected and ignored.

That was the beauty of Portugal for me. I knew that the laws of nature and the universe would be amplified there, creating a unique, resonant space where I could be present as I released what no longer served me.

Christine Patton

IN THE SACRED GROVE OF EPIDAURUS

My husband Dwight and I arrived at Epidaurus late afternoon in early September, two hours before closing time. Epidaurus is the biggest and most famous healing sanctuary of antiquity, established around 600 B.C. near the eastern coast of the Peloponnese peninsula in Greece. According to legends, Epidaurus was the burial place of Asklepios, the mythological father of the healing arts.

The scent of pine greeted us when we stepped out of the car. As we walked along the path, past the café, cross-hatched branches reached up toward the sky to form a canopy over our heads. Wherever I looked, tall trunks clustered like welcoming friends. Pine trees were considered special in ancient Greece and believed to be cleansing to their surroundings and healing for the body.

The site of the *asklepion*, or healing sanctuary, stretched through a clearing as we faced the vast remains of ancient temples, priests' quarters, sanatoria, hotels, baths, theaters, and a stadium. The sanctuary was huge, a combination of a modern-day hospital, spa, and gym. Across from the asklepion rose the most famous theater of the ancient world. It has perfect acoustics, unsurpassed even in our century, and is still used for performances of classical Greek plays.

On this visit, I didn't want to make detours to admire the beauty and acoustics of the theater; I knew exactly what I wanted to see at this sacred site. First the *tholos*. This mysterious, round structure stood at the heart of the sanctuary, in the sacred grove where death was banned. Although the asklepion was for the ancients what hospitals are for us today, no one was allowed to die while there. In the same spirit, women weren't permitted to give birth there. Without death and birth, there is only eternity, a conquest over human mortality. In this way, they thought men could assume the power of gods.

We walked silently past the priest's quarters and the Temple of Asklepios until we reached the far end of the sacred grove. In front of us crouched the enclosure of the tholos—actually only the basement of it, which is what remains of a once colonnaded, richly decorated, circular building. It was surprisingly small—and roped off to the public.

That late afternoon, Dwight carefully looked around for a guard, but there were hardly any tourists, let alone guards. He gave me a "go" with his head, and I jumped over the ropes and climbed down into the enclosure.

I found myself within the confines of concentric walls about six feet high, built of stone blocks and without a roof. As I started touring, I discovered what made this structure a miniature labyrinth: Each of the three walls had a narrow opening cut at a different angle. I went around in one direction, then around in the opposite direction, and around again until I reached the end—a tiny, circular room, the same height as the walls but capped by a wooden roof. It was just big enough for one person. This is where it is believed the priests kept the snakes they used in healing rituals. Snakes, together with dogs and roosters, were sacred animals to Asklepios. He was frequently depicted standing with a long wooden staff around which was entwined a large snake.

I gingerly stepped into the semi-darkness of the tiny room, my mind alert, senses like antennae, body taut like a bow. I was in the center of the labyrinth now, the underground part of the tholos—and now what?

How could I seek to be healed from this awful fatigue that had robbed my life of the very feeling of aliveness?

Just as the skeptical part of me was waking up, I had a download of thoughts and knew what to do. A healing ritual performed by facing the four directions was revealed to me. The South to shed the old, and then the East for a new birth. North to align myself with the magnetic field of Earth and finally West, to pay my respects to the forces of decay and death.

I began by facing the South and asking fervently that my body be cleansed of all parasites and germs, as well as any physical and emotional negativities that had caused this condition of constant fatigue. As I was visualizing streams of muck leaving my body, I felt tingling in the soles of my feet and a strong pull from below. It was as if a powerful vacuum cleaner was positioned beneath my feet and was sucking the crud down and out. While this was happening, an intense wave of heat started to climb up my legs and further into my body.

When I turned to face the East, I felt a surge of joy and elation as a shimmering, white energy field lifted me above my body. I merged with this loving, infinitely sweet energy. The feeling was unmistakable: This was the real me—my soul. I had experienced glimpses of this state on and off over the past years; I had sought to recreate it during long hours of meditation in the ashrams in India. The memory of its presence remained like a beacon on my path. And here it was now, scooping me up in its embrace like a mother holding her newborn baby. Gently, so gently. I felt infused with the energy of a new beginning.

I felt a prod, more like a command, to turn and face the North. As I did, the shimmering white began to fade. I tried desperately to seize that beautiful, loving energy, but the more I tried, the faster it vanished. I wanted to turn back to recapture the presence of my soul, but now I was rooted in the spot. The energy had changed.

Enveloped in a busy, agitated cloud, I felt tiny beings swoop down to adjust my body like a crew of mechanics fixing a race car at a pit stop. A thought appeared that this was necessary for healing, and I remained still and patient.

When the sensations subsided, I knew it was time to turn to the West and offer my gratitude.

Slowly, I walked out of the labyrinth and climbed back atop the enclosure wall. Dazed, I sat down next to Dwight and looked around. The hills, the pines, the fragments of columns strewn about—everything seemed luminous, faintly glowing with a light I had not noticed before. I felt perfectly poised, renewed, and strong. Every muscle vibrated with energy; my body throbbed with a stream of power that coursed through me like a mountain river.

As the dusk silently glided into the grove, bringing violet shades and air redolent with herbs, I inhaled deeply and felt vibrantly alive.

Svetlana Meritt

INITIATION

*W*e were the first to jump out of the bus. As Kalidah, Debbie, Tom, and I walked together from the parking lot across the sandy plateau of Giza, I remembered what Prema, my Egyptian temple dance teacher, had told me about the true purpose of the Great Pyramid of Cheops.

"Though there is a sarcophagus, they never found anyone buried inside," she had said. "Members of the true mystical traditions, both past and present, knew the Great Pyramid as a temple of initiation. As students of the mystery schools, they underwent long and intensive study and rituals to purify and balance their physical, emotional, and spiritual energies. Then, after years of training and many tests, the instructors escorted the initiates deep within the pyramid to the king's chamber for their final initiation."

Prema was part of the lineage extending back to these mystery schools, and my studies with her were preparing me for a similar destiny. I hoped to experience the transformative power of the king's chamber.

Our guide handed us our tickets to enter the Great Pyramid. Climbing through the grand foyer to the king's chamber tested my resolve. Already disillusioned by the crowds of people, I ducked, then crouched, then bent double to avoid hitting my head as I moved further into the interior. I began to feel the pressure of all the stones bearing down on me. Although I'm not usually claustrophobic, I started hyperventilating.

Entering the king's chamber, I stood squashed up against the wall. People jabbered and joked all around us. I'd come so far, and now, with all the inane comments, we could have been in a shopping mall. The chattering tourists weren't cooperating with my desire for a deep, spiritual experience.

Slowly, people began to filter out of the chamber, and I was left alone with my traveling companions. I stood quietly and waited for the next onslaught of tourists, but none came.

I leaned against the wall and slowly slipped down the smooth stones, coming to rest on the floor. The hard rock against my bottom grounded me. Closing my eyes, I felt the walls begin to pulsate. I could hear a faint sound of voices that turned into a chant, which grew louder and louder. The sound became a deafening roar and the heaviness of the millions of tons of stone above me created an almost unbearable pressure. I felt energy traveling up and down my spine. The thunderous sound rattled my bones, turning my backbone into a tuning fork. The dissonant chord built to a crescendo, and then the top of my head felt like it exploded, unleashing a blinding light.

My eyes flashed open. The stone walls were transparent. I was sitting in a pyramid of crystal white light and experienced myself as pure energy. I'd been here forever and would continue into eternity.

I could see the desert before the pyramid was built. I watched the structure rise from the sand as thousands of builders labored over its creation. I observed the rituals of other awakening initiates, the terror and the freedom of those who went beyond their rational minds.

I saw the centuries when the pyramid disappeared, covered first by the floodwaters and later by sand. I sensed the excitement of those who saw it again for the first time. I witnessed an endless stream of visitors making their way through this chamber. The string of visions unfolded for eons. I was the consciousness of the pyramid itself, experiencing its history.

Slowly, I became conscious of Kalidah, Debbie, and Tom. We were still alone in the king's chamber. I could see from the expressions in their wide-open eyes that they, too, had experienced something astonishing. At that moment, I knew we had been destined to come and sit opposite each other within these four walls. Together, we created a chord, a sound that fixed the pattern of our experience.

Hearing others approach, we rose in unison and crawled silently out of the pyramid. Back on the bus, our tour group went to a restaurant where the four of us sat quietly together. At first, we were each lost in our own worlds.

Eventually, we began speaking at once. "What happened? What did you see? What did it mean?"

We questioned each other excitedly. The content of our experiences wasn't the same, but we'd each encountered a transcendent, all-consuming light. Gathered around the table in that crowded restaurant, we shared our feelings of kinship with this land and the ancient religion and rituals that revolved around preparing to live through eternity in a glorious afterworld. Our experiences in the pyramid confirmed we were following trails that reached beyond our present existence.

Sherry Brier

THE PETRIFIED ANGEL

*R*aw energy may not be for everyone, yet there are times when a situation calls for its application, regardless of one's gender. Energy is a tool like any other, and the experienced mystic knows when the application of force is required above subtlety. Raw energy can shock us out of a predicament, or transmute stagnation, or remove a block to enable the life force to resume its normal course.

Tsé Bit'a'í is the sacred place of the Navajo, and before them, the Anasazi. Its raw, unfiltered power commands respect. It is entrancing. The sense of temporal space quickly evaporates, along with fear, anger, and any heavy baggage you might bring to this desert landscape. Whenever I am drawn here I always leave lighter of heart and strangely healed of whatever is afflicting me, not that I come to dump my problems—one should always avoid doing so, as it pollutes the balanced environment of sacred space.

I am perfectly happy to meditate at the base of Tsé Bit'a'í and be taken to where this petrified angel needs to take me, expecting nothing in return. On my virgin visit, there was not a soul to be seen, and you can see very far in every direction. I drank the stillness and imbibed the fragrance of desert sage, only then to hear people dancing in ceremony around me. Then I *saw* people dancing around me. I am not a dancer, I despise dancing, but a force compelled me to rise and join the circling crowd. Not knowing more than three words in Navajo, I joined in the chant.

The sun had just set. The temperature dropped in unison and I suddenly felt the cold air. I was again alone with the stillness. Nothing moved. Nor did I wish to move, but with light fading fast, it was imperative to leave or be lost to the night, the trails in the reservation are worn and confusing.

I felt I was taught something that evening. Soon after I would meet the Zuni elder, the late and great Clifford Mahooty, who would assist me in my quest to understand Native American culture in the way only it understands, the knowledge of which formed the foundation of my second book. Not that I knew I would be writing a book, but clearly, someone out there already knew and put me in touch with Clifford.

Years later I traveled to the site again with my partner who was visiting from New Zealand. The site was well out of the way from our intended itinerary, yet I sensed it calling to bring her, and knowing her the way I did, I understood why. Without being aware of a single thing about the background of Tsé Bit'a'í, she was adamant about wanting to climb the near vertical breccia and did so despite my protestations. But she insisted and proceeded regardless.

Half an hour later, she returned, shaken to the core.

The site is a useful tool with which to conquer fear, and it will force you to face your own, for without this crucial step your spiritual development remains stunted.

Ultimately, I'm not certain if she ever took this lesson on board, but this story demonstrates how portals do not exist to fix you, they merely provide the *potential* to do so. The rest, as they say, is up to you.

Tsé Bit'a'í is about as humbling an experience as I've ever had at a portal.

Freddy Silva

PART THREE

Interacting with Portals

Behind all seen things lies something vaster; everything is but a path, a portal or a window opening on something other than itself.

— ANTOINE DE SAINT-EXUPERY

HOW TO ENGAGE WITH PORTALS

W hen deciding to erect a church on virgin soil, early Celtic Christian monks would observe the behavior of animals, particularly cows, when they were about to give birth. When a cow in labor experiences difficulty, it breaks out of its enclosure, walks about the pasture as though searching for something, and once found, the cow moves in ever decreasing circles, crouches, and brings to the light a calf.

Animals know all there is to know when it comes to sourcing the subtle force of nature to assist them to navigate life and its speed bumps. Animals are the ultimate *source-rers*, keen practitioners of *at-one-ment*.

Assuming you do not possess the honing skills of a cow, coyote or crow—although they exist in everyone—you need guidance when interacting with portals.

I've been fortunate to have had erudite teachers along my journey, coupled with sufficient experience working with ancient sacred places to offer candid advice. Now that I (hopefully) know more than I did when I was a piece of gum attached to the sole of the sandal of a guru, I can honestly say the interaction with energetically active places has developed my *inner tuition,* while my sensitivity has sharpened to the point where others may feel uncomfortable.

Looking back at events in my life, I possessed these abilities all along, there just was no one around to tell me what they were or guide me to direct them to where they could be applied. Families and friends regarded me as a square peg in the round hole of society, their discomfort disguised by avoiding my work and instead discussing the weather. Only when the right teacher appeared did my progress begin in earnest. But then, had I not been ready, consciously or otherwise, I would still be tethered to a frustrating day job and reluctantly fitting into a society far removed from the world discussed so far.

So, allow me to pour out what I know when it comes to interacting with the *spots of the fawn.*

EXPECTATION

All the experiences and traditions mentioned throughout this work are magical, yes, but when it comes to a portal there is one caveat: approach it with the expectation of experiencing something earth shattering and it won't happen. Like driving an hour to your favorite restaurant only to discover it closed on Tuesdays, the disappointment is hard to swallow.

Expectation is the handmaid of desire.

If you expect enlightenment in a temple, a vision in a sacred place, or a paragraph of advice from a portal, you *might* get it, yes, because it will come from your need for fulfilment. It will come from your own mind. You paid a lot of money to travel to temple X or sacred mountain Y, and you expect a return on your investment. In my experience, that approach never turns out well.

When I was learning to dowse, I was astonished at how easy it was to achieve instant results. Every time. A natural born rod man. Until a real dowser suggested that most of my results were coming from my need for validation. It wasn't a case of cheating so much as trying too hard, forcing the outcome; the rods twitched and obliged. The remedy was simple: *Let go of expectation, clear the mind, be honest with myself.* Honest enough to throw away two years of dowsing maps of sacred sites.

Pride swallowed, I spent another two years relearning everything, interacting with subtle energy to such a degree that dowsing became second nature, my body became so attuned to telluric currents that I no longer need copper rods or pendulums. Now I can *see* energy, its direction of flow, its gender, and in rare occurrences, its color.

Expectation played a key role in my first visit to Egypt as a member of Isabelle the Medium's group. The journey's goal was to develop our latent abilities by experiencing different forms of energy inherent at various sites. Every temple was designed for a different purpose, as was every pyramid. They might look the same, but subtleties in geometry and proportion infuse each one with a different quality, which in turn influences your temporal state of awareness.

The Great Pyramid is the repose of intense, masculine energy. It can be disconcerting, not everyone's cup of tea. For reasons unknown we failed to secure private access for the entire group; only six of us were allowed to enter, and then forced to share the building with members of the public, which led to another lesson: acceptance of fate (also known in general circles as *disappointment*).

Screeching children, humidity, musty odor from perspiring armpits, low and cumbersome passages—I didn't know what I'd expected but it certainly wasn't this and found my annoyance rising at the lack of respect the building deserves.

We persevered up the Grand Gallery, toward the King's Chamber and its perfectly bonded, megalithic granite blocks showcasing the ancient world's fluent ability to work the hardest stone on Earth like putty. The crowd thinned. The two women in our group felt uncomfortable and exited the chamber, leaving the remaining four of us alone in a silent chamber, an incredible stroke of luck.

Unusual things began to happen. The cacophonous compressor in the contraption that passed for an air conditioner stopped. The lights switched off. Immersed in darkness, we agreed to assist in clearing and rejuvenating the energy of the building, which is sadly neglected from time to time. The technique involves defining a focus and using the sound of the voice to carry an envelope of energy to an intended location, making good use of the millions of particles of quartz in the stone for the intent to soak into the fabric of the building. Called *toning*, it works much in the same way one pushes a button on a computer that sends an electric signal to the circuit board which instructs a silicon chip (quartz) to execute an action.

I shifted around in the dark to find the sweet spot in the coal black chamber, about a third of the way back from the box that is mistaken for a sarcophagus. A sinuous feeling between body and building overcame me, and sounds—the likes of which I had never made before or since—came out of my throat. As the others joined in, the natural acoustics brewed our voices into an intoxicating melody.

It was at this point that my life and my perception of portals changed forever. Emanating from the granite walls, a group of tall people, all dressed in long, white gowns, encircled us. I still remember turning my head to look at them in the total darkness. There must have been thirty or so. They lowered their heads and I lowered mine in respect. It felt like a reunion with a long lost family, and I did not want them to go, my head was filled with many questions.

I don't recall how many minutes the interaction lasted, it didn't matter, we were in a conclave with magic.

No sooner had we stopped toning when the two light bulbs flickered back to life. I looked at the others, and although no words were exchanged,

I knew each of these people had also experienced something profound. The sound of an agitated Arab voice hailed from somewhere deep below. We'd probably overstayed our welcome and made haste.

In the bright desert light, we exchanged glances, it was obvious we wanted to say something, so I initiated.

"Did you see what I saw up there?"

"You mean the people, in a circle, all in white?"

You can't fake moments like this. Unless you want to and your imagination obliges. Before this life changing experience, I had no idea such an interaction was even possible. I was still learning.

We rejoined the group, who'd resorted to experiencing the Great Pyramid from the outside, using remote sensing to look within, and before any of us shared our experience, Isabelle said, "Well, that was fun, wasn't it? You went there with the right intent, honored the site, and the guardians came out of the stones."

It would not be the first or final time I engaged with these unusual people. As my experience and confidence grew, I began to lead my own groups, with a guided meditation in the King's Chamber as the culmination of weeks experiencing different temples, and with them, the discernment of different forms of energy. Twice I've seen the Shining Ones emerge from the stones. What was amazing about the second experience was how a third of the group picked up on them, vividly, without any prompting; most were not even familiar with my own experience.

Since then, I've realized these guardians have been guiding the direction of much of my work. That's quite a relationship.

The important point here is that I did not travel to Egypt with expectation. Nothing I experienced was the result of a craving for special blessing or a validation of my spiritual needs. I went as a blank canvas and the cosmos impressed itself upon me.

PREPARATION

Location, location, location is sound advice when it comes to selling property. The motto for approaching sacred space is *preparation, preparation, preparation.*

Before approaching a portal, ask yourself, *What is it that I'm looking for? What is the purpose of this interaction?*

Be succinct and honest, feel it, be passionate with your request, but place no attachment on the outcome.

Now that intent is established, don't dwell on it, let it go.

Since humans and portals share two basic ingredients—electricity and magnetism—focused intent takes on the form of a packet of energy moving through time and space, and as it does, so its content is picked up and read by every portal on the planet. And beyond; in fact, since the electrical impulse of thought travels instantaneously, the moment an intention is formulated, every portal knows about it even before the signal is intellectualized by the brain.

What happens next might take you by surprise. Just as you're packing your bags for Egypt, plans go awry and you end up in Scotland. Your mind and your desire *expected* the answer to be Egypt, but your subconscious, who knows better, was busy in a back room negotiating on your behalf with every portal, to which a Scottish stone circle responded, *I have exactly what you requested. See you in a week.*

You might come across hundreds of menhirs, dolmens, and pyramids, but remember: each is an individual in its own right; each is imbued with a set of subtleties, each designed to fulfill a specific purpose. If there's a match, a connection is established and the relationship begins.

You so desperately wanted to climb Pyramid IV in Tikal because it is featured in Star Wars VI, but instead you were guided to Pyramid VII where, for some bizarre reason, you spent two hours—all by yourself. And the download you received turned out to be exactly the information required.

The intent for my first Egyptian experience was to learn the true nature of the sites and be a better teacher. I meant it, and embodied it in my own peculiar shorthand: *What's this all about?*

And look at what and where it got me.

One further piece of advice. As strange as it may seem, what you eat is an important aspect of preparation. Because you are about to engage with an environment where worlds interpenetrate, the denser your vibration, the more difficulty you will have accessing the Otherworld. Fasting for a day or two does wonders for your state of awareness in sacred space. I may be a carnivore at heart, but when I want to engage with a portal, two pieces of fruit and a bottle of water is all I need to sustain me. A lighter body provides greater clarity in my immediate spatial environment and my mind is able to process information with less interference.

Some people choose to fast for a week or longer, particularly those involved with initiation and out-of-body journeying. The lighter the physical body, the less resistance the soul encounters as it attempts to leave. However, this aspect of working with a portal is far more specialized and beyond the scope of this book to explain in minute detail.

In a nutshell, the rules for preparation are:

Set intention.

Get on with your life.

Expect nothing.

Fast.

Be surprised.

APPROACHING THE PORTAL

Because it is an aggregate of living energy, a portal is sensitive to the quality of input. Energy is energy. It does not care one way or the other about right or wrong action. If the input is positive, the portal expands and maintains itself in equilibrium, much like a flower bud opens in reaction to sunlight.

The opposite also holds true. The abuse of a site saps its energy, and if repeated, it becomes lifeless, with a negative environment to boot. There's an ancient mound in southwest England that once was a site of great veneration, but as the weathervane of politics changed direction it was adapted into a notorious prison—*a most annoying, contagious and detestable place within this realm*, as local residents described it. Sensible to give this site a wide berth, you might say, but I use it as a test for people to understand what it feels like to experience the total absence of light and love. Thirty-five seconds is the longest anyone lasts before running out of the building, with their skin taking on a sickly pallor.

The point is this: When approaching sacred space, do not take your problems inside. The site is a living, breathing organism. Put yourself in its place, would you enjoy listening to your whining for hours? The burden you bring is a bundle of energy whose negative signature will imprint itself, polluting an otherwise balanced environment, leaving the next visitor to wonder why the space feels somewhat diminished.

A portal is not an agony aunt, although some treat it as such, yet it takes little effort to adapt a positive spin. Rather than approach with a burden you hope to alleviate, turn the idea on its head.

I seek clarity with an issue.

I seek empowerment to overcome an impediment.

With this approach, the interaction with sacred space serves to transmute a situation, and you become a co-participant in the process.

And of course, let go of expectation.

The entrance to the great court of Saqqara in Egypt is an excellent example of how temple architects manipulated telluric currents to act as a force field, protecting the temple from unbalanced thoughts and emotions. The attentive visitor today will feel as though pushed and pulled when walking down the colonnade of stone reeds, because the alcoves separating the columns emit alternating positive and negative currents. As these currents act on the body, the visitor is reminded to leave their problems outside the temple and not pollute the sensitive environment within.

MINDFULNESS

Minding thoughts and emotions is a basic exercise to employ before putting on a coat and walking out of the house to your portal.

As I approach sacred space, if the situation allows, I like to walk clockwise around its perimeter (counterclockwise in the southern hemisphere) to open its energy field. Yes, sacred sites open and close, just like we work and rest; when closed, the energy remains within, but with reduced output. The opening process has an added advantage: by consciously engaging with the portal's protective energy field, you become mindful of it. The interaction is no longer illusional but tangible.

Some choose to walk the site singing or playing musical instruments, or with herbs and incense; in ancient Egypt, priests would shut down each room of a temple at sunset, only to return before sunrise and tone in each room as though waking a person from slumber. There is no hard and fast rule here, yet such simple exercises help you engage consciously with the spirit of place, who then acknowledges the effort you've taken to respect the site.

Once immersed in sacred space, your thoughts inevitably lead your mind in all directions. Then there are visual distractions to take you further away from your intended goal, and before you know it, you've spent a few good hours walking the site yet not fully engaged. The experience could have been better served.

Working with sacred space requires you to be present, and paradoxically, not present. The ideal is to find yourself in a state between asleep and awake, one foot in the physical, the other in the ethereal. And it does not require ingesting drugs, in fact, they only get in the way.

When I was taking spiritual development classes, I was taught a very simple technique to make you acutely mindful of your environment. To become *sensitive*, as it were. As I sat down, I was asked, "Name ten sounds you heard before entering the room?"

"Er…car engine…traffic…."

Blank.

"Now, go for a walk and return in fifteen minutes and think about what I said."

Fifteen minutes later. *Front door closing, gravel underfoot, the caw of a crow, sheep in the distance, wind moving leaves, rustle of tall grass, bubbling of stream behind hedgerow, wet barley crackling in the sunlight, laundry flapping on a line, buzz of electric cable, donkey munching hay, tinkle of glass from delivering milkman, bird pecking a window…*

And just like that I was mindful of my surroundings. Repeat this in any sacred space and you'll be amazed at how quickly you can learn to perceive the invisible universe with your inner eye. And from there, to physically see the hidden universe, just the way a psychic does.

The technique is especially valuable in an open landscape where portals are unmarked by standing stones or temples. The atmosphere inside a portal feels denser, like liquid that isn't wet; the movement of air alters the sonic quality of the immediate surroundings; a tingling sensation is felt on fingertips or the inner palm of the hand. All these sensations can be experienced with your enhanced sensitivity. Practiced again and again your awareness expands and inevitably draws you to that special spot you are searching for.

I recall a special day walking down a vale looking for a portal on Temple Farm, near Marlborough, England. As the name implies, it was owned by the Templars. Alongside Isabelle the Medium, we searched for a site we'd been asked to activate. The area is unremarkable—the odd thorn bush or hedge here and there, but amid this sparseness, we stopped as though on cue. We felt that density of air, the muffled sound: we were standing in the portal. All it took was focused intent and mindfulness, nothing more.

Perhaps my favorite tool is the camera. Looking through the viewfinder helps me become acutely aware of fine details, particularly in sacred places. God is in the details, as they say. But more importantly, it stops my mind chattering, I become fully immersed in my surroundings and nothing distracts me. Before I know it, hours have slipped by, and mindfulness has led me to write new material.

On the many occasions I visited Cuzco, I felt compelled to experience a different part of this beautiful, ancient city in the Andes. One day I attended the local covered market, which I'd learned had originally been a pre-Inka temple. The floor is all that remains, its megaliths highly polished by thousands of feet rubbing it every day in search of all kinds of household wares. The place is bustling and cacophonous and difficult to maintain concentration, compounded by the overwhelming sights and smells of a foreign world. But with my camera and a passion for that very difficult technique, candid photography, I was no longer in the market, I was *immersed* in the market, halfway between asleep and awake, fully aware but not thinking.

I stopped at one unremarkable spot where I felt as though wrapped inside a whirlpool of energy rising out of the floor. I just stood there, enraptured, drinking this potent yet tranquil vortex while shown some vivid imagery to assist my ongoing research of the region. Vaguely aware of Peruvians jostling around me, I looked across at a woman pouring beans into a small bag. She gave the biggest smile, and said, in Spanish, "You feel it, too? It's beautiful, isn't it? That's why we set up at this spot, it is *muy especial.*"

"*Si, muy especial,*" I agreed.

The older lady sitting across the way, knitting, nodded in agreement.

Energized, I met up with Edgar, my Aymara guide, who said, "I want to show you an old temple, now the market, I know you will like it, it has a special energy in one location... but looks like you probably found it already?"

"*Si.*"

These are just some techniques for achieving mindfulness. I've seen people use meditation, tai chi, yoga, music, prayer, reading, tantric sex (no, really), the list goes on. And since there is no exact method, it is imperative you find the one best suited to your personality.

Experiment, play.

LOOK FOR PORTALS IN UNCOMMON PLACES

Roald Dahl once accurately observed, *Watch with glittering eyes the whole world around you because the greatest secrets are always hidden in the most unlikely places.*

In nature, all form follows function, and where earth energy is particularly potent, nature appears more abundant as it follows the path of least resistance. Thus in Britain, it is not uncommon for a portal to be defined by a cluster of trees growing in a ring, in essence giving physical shape to an invisible ripple in the local energy field. The same is true of geology, it adapts and shapes itself according to a subtle underlying force. When searching for a portal, it pays to be mindful when walking the land searching for signs, particularly those to which you might be unexpectedly attracted. This cluster of stones or that unusual bend in the river, more often than not, is the physical expression of an unseen force. Beauty may be bait to the eye, but behind it lives an expression of energy in equilibrium. Conversely, a row of dying trees amid an otherwise healthy forest signals a spot where the life force is depleted. We are drawn to the former not so much because of its visual appeal but because it contains the ingredients necessary for the subconscious and the soul to connect with a pool of nourishment.

Since they exist across the entire planet, you don't need to wait to travel abroad before engaging with a portal. There's one in my living room. There may be one in a lawn or a city park where you live. Incredible as it may seem, that sense of connection experienced on a holy hill in Ireland is also to be found in the urban environment of Manhattan. In Central Park, a large boulder scratched by the weight of a retreating ice shelf happens to occupy a geomagnetic hotspot where one can happily be away with the faeries for hours.

In fact, amid the bustle of New York, certain benches, cafes, museums, and galleries carry an aura of enchantment, because they were deliberately put there by someone who was mindful of the underlying energy of the land. A town planner placed an obelisk on that spot because it *felt* right. A gut feeling guided a gardener to shape a hedge like an arc with a fountain at the center. These people perceived *the spots of the fawn*.

Then there are others who were consciously aware of their actions. Midtown Manhattan is a utopia for lovers of Art Deco. It is not unusual to discover that the architects of spaces in and around Grand Central Station or Rockefeller Center or the Chrysler Building were involved with Scottish Rite Freemasonry, whose ethos stems directly from the teachings of *Tayi* and the Mysteries schools of ancient Egypt. The aim of such fraternities was the elevation of the human condition amid a discombobulated industrial society. In doing so, they behaved like our ancestors when they selected their sacred caves. They provided an antidote, channeling a natural resource for the wellbeing of society, just as society was losing track of its relationship to the land. Hence why I refer to a portal as a *self-help center*. It is an insurance policy for maintaining sanity, the cable that restores me to who I really am.

Ten minutes from my home, there is a beach I walk to recharge. It is not necessarily the prettiest part of the coast, nor does it attract great attention.

But at low tide, it is the one spot among three square miles of sand and stone to which I gravitate when my soul is out of alignment and seeks to reconnect. The body knows what it needs to bring itself into equilibrium, it seeks the portal for proper balance.

I just obey and follow. Soon, my soul is replenished, and my battery is full.

RESPECT

Which brings me to another rule: thank the spirit of place every time. It will be the best extended family you'll want to spend time with, because it never lets you down. Just don't take it for granted.

TIMING

When is it going to happen?

The world of spirit is amused by our relentless impatience.

It is important to understand that the human construct of time bears no resemblance beyond our planet. Time is wholly suited to this three-dimensional sphere and the satisfaction of commerce. I've observed how cultures who do not rely on wristwatches are the happiest because they function at the speed of nature, and thus they adapt to its whims with greater flexibility than a Wall Street trader.

Time is relative.

To ask the spirit world *when* will the vision come, *when* will I get an answer, *when* will manifestation of my intent occur, is a pointless and futile exercise in frustration. Their best answer is an educated guess because the spirit world functions along a different set of parameters.

They are immortal, we are time sensitive.

Manifestation is also relative to your level of development. Handling knowledge for which you are ill-equipped makes life frustrating; worse, it deprives you of the lesson for which you chose to incarnate: experience.

Like driving, if you haven't first read the manual, you won't locate the ignition, and the expensive machine you bought leaves you stranded. Sometimes you *think* you know where to insert the key, but the first turn onto the road you crash the car into an unyielding object because you haven't taken a single driving lesson.

Be patient, all good things happen when they're supposed to. I've been handed information at sacred places that manifest anywhere between immediately to a year after the event, and it all appeared exactly when I needed it, not at the speed my ego demanded. Certain things needed to be learned before I understood what was placed on my plate. Not that it stopped my complaining, but then, in the highway of three-dimensional life, we're all learners.

Bear in mind that you are also a cog in a large machine and the cogs need to line up before forward motion can occur. Patience and acceptance are key to getting the most from the invisible universe. This does not mean you stop living by sitting on a chair and staring out of the window. The universe owes you nothing and no one is entitled to anything. Simply continue to work toward your goal, even if the horizon is nothing but a bank of fog, because the universe will meet you halfway, and when it does, the current moves very, very rapidly.

SYMPATHETIC RESONANCE

There is a big difference between *May the force be with you* and *Use the force to force a result*.

The creative force behind the universe is filled with potential, thus what you receive from a portal depends on what it is you're asking. Words, actions and intentions all carry resonance, and like any functional relationship, that resonance seeks to find a partner with whom to dance.

I've experienced some wondrous portals in my time, and often, I gained nothing more than the pleasure of their company. Or to quote Sting, *Some gods did not make a sound.*

Early on, my engagement with portals was often met with silence, no matter how hard I squinted, waiting for magic to happen. *Oh, the disappointment.* Why? Because there was no sympathetic resonance between the portal and my requirement. It could not provide me with what I was searching for, yet kind enough to send me along to another location where the resonance was a better match. Magic ensued.

If you're on the mystical path, then you know that each encounter raises your resonance, because your body absorbs each new vibration. Conversely, if your vibration is not in sympathy with the temple, the result can be discomforting. In serious cases, the interaction can make you sick. It's the temple's way of warning you that what you are about to experience is not in your best interests. In such cases it is best to heed the warning, move on, and find a temple where you are instantly at ease.

During my years in Wiltshire I lived near one of its oldest sites, an eroded passage mound renamed Devil's Den by the usual suspects. It sits in a shallow valley surrounded by open meadow and pasture. On my first visit I was stunned to hear a deep voice telling me, *Do not approach this place.* With my leg midair as I climbed a wire fence, I thought the farmer had caught me, even though the site is accessible to the public. *I'm imagining things. Onwards.* But there it was again: *You will come no further.* And whoever it was meant it.

Sheepishly I retraced my steps along the overgrown footpath and returned to my car.

A few minutes later, I dropped by to have tea with Isabelle. As she boiled the kettle, without me saying a word, she remarked, "Have you just come back from the Devil's Den? Did you get the voice?"

You can't fake stuff like this. "Er… yes."

"That place is raw power. You still have a way to go with learning. Give it a couple of years, then go back and see what happens," she replied.

Two years later and more experience under my belt, I took a second stab at Devil's Den. It was like night and day, as though a red carpet extended all the way into the chamber. I felt the embrace of welcome from the spirit of place. I had raised my resonance to match the portal. I had elevated my game, and better equipped, I was ready to tackle the next level of frequency.

Ancient mystics employed various techniques to make the best of their interaction with portals. There is a chamber in the Valley of the Kings in Egypt where, uncharacteristically, no one is buried. It is an anomaly and deliberately so, for it invites the seeker to question what it is doing in a valley otherwise dedicated to physical death.

Egyptian mystics understood the difference between physical death and metaphoric death, and to be better equipped during incarnation they conducted a dangerous ritual whereby the candidate was given a poison and the soul left the body to experience the Otherworld, typically for three days. They undertook this perilous journey because of the tangible benefits it provided upon returning to the body, those being true knowledge of the mechanics of nature and the universe. *True philosophers make dying their living*, as Greek commentators would later remark.

The instructions on the curved wall of Thutmosis III's chamber state, *Whoever understands these mysterious images is a well-provided light being, always able to enter and leave the Otherworld.* The point was to make good use of the portal to gain understanding of celestial mechanics and the soul's place in the bigger scheme of things. By understanding who you truly are and the clarity of your purpose, your time on Earth is better spent, you gain mastery of the process of manifestation, and in doing so, develop a degree of control of the unseen road across the horizon.

You become a well-provided light being on that strange adventure called *Life*.

GIVE. AND TAKE

Finally, people often wonder how temples that were built thousands of years ago still manage to retain their presence. It's simple. You have a five-year-old fern in your living room, why is it still alive? Because you watered it for five years.

The replenishment of energy first comes from the design and location of a site in direct contact with the earth's electromagnetic wiring, which in turn is recharged by the Sun. The process is then amplified by enthusiasts, wisdom-keepers, well-wishers, and adepts who sustain it across millennia.

A living energy field is a bundle of *e-motion*—energy in motion—and like you, it reacts favorably to positive attention: a thought of appreciation, a prayer, an offering, a drop of your own inner light, ritual, even a nod of acknowledgement is all it takes to maintain a site in perpetuity. When you interact with sacred space you are literally imbibing the residual affirmations and goodwill of those who came before.

Use a portal to take inventory. And to replenish inventory.

In other words, don't approach merely with the intention of taking. Give something back. Feed it. Taking without replenishing leaves nothing but sterile soil.

Even if all you get from a portal is the satisfaction of engaging with a world barely a breath away, go, engage. Who knows, like ancient Egyptian initiates claimed, you might be transformed into a well-provided light being.

SPRINGBOARD INTO
THE UNKNOWN
———— ℈+℈ ————

a portal is a point of possibility, a step into a thousand journeys.

A springboard from the known into the unknown.

There's a wonderful paradox here. We incarnate from the invisible universe to experience an unknown world—Earth—yet spend much of the experience on Earth making sense of the known by seeking answers in the unknown. It is the stuff of Zen.

If we accept that accessing a portal allows for the discovery of our origins, it follows that the memory of what is retrieved will assist us in understanding the plan we have chosen to follow. For this to occur, we must step out of the cocoon and dabble in a parallel reality.

My position lies with our ancient predecessors who lived a rudimentary existence without the need to overcomplicate or intellectualize the universe. Mental acrobatics might impress others but will only leave you with an *approximate* grasp of reality. You will have the picture frame but not the picture.

The temporal human world is fickle, flexible and merciless. An immersion with magic allows for the transformation of our existence into an expression of sacred space. It is more effective than oxygen. People like Plato and Philip the Apostle were right, one gains far more insight when engaging with those special places that transport you into the Otherworld. Even a brush with the miraculous is enough to fuel the resolve required to make each waking day a moment worth savoring. I know it to be good advice because such experiences have buoyed me on my journey of incarnation, a journey whose challenges, disappointments and pains would have killed most people by now.

And yet, like the green man, here I am.

Still.

It is early morning outside Minster church in Cornwall, set amid an atmospheric, moss covered wood. It was once the site of Talkarn, a rock-cut chapel, home to a Gaelic holy man who chose it for the telluric currents flowing through the site, and ever since, it's been a place for mystics wishing to engage with a parallel universe.

It is so piercingly quiet that Isabelle, along with another psychic and friend, Jane, and I can hear the mellifluous trickling of water from the nearby spring. We've come to drink the essence of this ancient place of veneration huddled in a steep valley above the fishing village of Boscastle.

The dank aroma inside the old church lends itself to quiet contemplation. Isabelle suggests we offer a dedication to the spirit of place and engage in toning. As usual, she dedicates her offering to the archangel Michael; Jane offers hers to Gabriel. As for me, I am tired from a long drive, and I flippantly offer mine to Saint Cecilia.

"Good choice," remarks Isabelle.

"Surely there is no such thing as Saint Cecilia," I reply.

"Are you kidding? She's only the patron saint of music," says Jane.

The gods just spanked me.

Interspersed in a triangle throughout the nave, we tone for a good ten minutes, the natural acoustics of the building blend our three voices into an opulent choir.

As often happens, the lights go out.

Making our way to the oak front door, I glance over at the ornate stained-glass window. "What are the chances! The three people we just dedicated are represented in the window."

All mouths are ajar.

Indeed, framed in the gothic arch stand three tall, vitrified figures, a sacred triptych. And for the rest of the day we are rightfully pleased with ourselves and our talent for connecting with the miraculous.

The following year, Jane and I return with another person, keen to relive the experience. But as we enter the church, something is amiss. I look up at the arch where the stained-glass window should be, but there is nothing—just ordinary, clear, leaded glass. *Perhaps the window was damaged in a storm.*

Quite by chance, the priest appears. I explain the situation that took place a year before. The priest looks at me with the warmth of a chisel.

"Never in the history of the church has there ever been a stained-glass window in that wall, or any wall," and storms away.

I inspect the caulking. He's right, there's no sign of a recent refurbishment, even the fungus looks old.

Puzzled, we walk to the village to seek expert advice from the researcher Paul Broadhurst. There's little about the history of every sacred place in this wind-beaten corner of Albion of which he is not aware. "No, there's no record of any stained glass in that church, and certainly not in recent times."

The mystery deepens. Only one other witness can confirm that Jane and I are not certifiable. We phone Isabelle.

"Do you remember that trip to Boscastle last year?"

"Oh yes, that thing with the angels and St. Cecilia in the stained-glass window. That was a good laugh, wasn't it?"

"There is no window. There has never been a window."

In the silence over the phone, one could hear the mellifluous steam rising from her tea.

MEET THE SACRED STORYTELLERS

ANNWYN'S awareness of the non-physical dimensions occurred in 2000, triggered by the death of her teen son, Tim. Under Tim's and others' guidance, she is now in service to Source. As well as channeling sacred sound as a planetary portal activator, Annwyn also teaches and activates others through writing, webinars, and workshops. annwynvibe.com.

SHERRY BRIER is the founder and director of Women Rock Project. She is the author of *Doorway to Ecstasy: A Dancer's Initiation* and *Daring Dazzling Divine: Secrets to Rock Your Life.*

MARY-ELIZABETH BRISCOE, LCMHC, CAGCS is the founder of Integrated Grief Works, LLC and the award-winning author of *The First Signs of April: A Memoir* on grief and healing.

SUE BRYAN, PH.D. is an author and self-actualization coach. She lives and writes in Santa Fe, New Mexico finding her inspiration in the high desert air.

KATHLEEN DALE lives with gratitude and appreciation for all that life offers and supports others in finding that path for themselves.

MICHAELA DAURIEL is a visual artist, storyteller, and mystical explorer with exceptional passion for Druidry, inner alchemy, sacred feminine, and underground realms.

SIA-LANU ESTRELLA is the author and channel of the internationally acclaimed Rainbow Tablets books. Australian-born, she has lived in the Peruvian Andes and United Kingdom. Her global retreats, mystery school, and sacred embodiment programs empower clients to unlock their cosmic wisdom and live in multidimensional mastery. sialanuestrella.com.

MARGUERITE HAFEMAN grew up in Colorado and received a MS of Science from Penn State. Career interests include commercial horticulturist, writer and editor, bookkeeper, certified astrologer, and tarot reader. She has had a lifetime interest in occult studies and spiritual development and is an avid student of archeoastronomy. mysticmarguerite.com.

REV. TERRI ANN HEIMAN, Reiki master teacher, spiritual counselor, and soul reader helps women in crisis build a spiritual practice to regain their confidence and trust their inner guidance. She is the author of *Confessions of a Shower Tapper – The Ultimate Guide to Living Your Purpose with EFT*, and host of *The Empowered Spirit Show*. terriannheiman.com.

THEA HOLLETT is a healer, channel, and writer. She has traveled and studied in many different lands and cultures–most notably, the Tibetans, the Maya, and the local indigenous of Canada. Thea currently lives in Canada and works with Quetzalcoatl, a Mayan ascended master. theahollett.com.

KERRY LYONS has had a lifelong interest in how the world works, and how it is to be in the world. Inevitably this led her to exploring the mystic realms, both intellectually and experientially.

IVY MEGAN is a medicine woman, psychic medium, area CE-5 coordinator, and holistic therapist. Her soul's purpose in this lifetime is to share wisdom and teachings she has gained through her spiritual journey, assisting others to reconnect with themselves at a deep soul level to remember who they are as an infinite being.

SVETLANA MERITT was a foreign correspondent before she went on a journey of self-discovery. She is the author of a spiritual travelogue *Meet Me in the Underworld: How 77 Sacred Sites, 770 Cappuccinos, and 26000 Miles Led Me to My Soul*.

IDA RA NALBANDIAN is the author of *Does God Have a Bicycle*, and *Jacob's Magic Vegetables*. Ida and her family founded VSCF-Vahagn Setian Charitable Foundation in memory of her late son, whose life was tragically cut short by a drunk driver. The foundation's mission is to promote self-awareness, attentive choices, and expand the greater good. vahagnfoundation.org.

PAMELA NANCE, MA has researched the survival of consciousness after death for over 30 years, holds certification in healing touch, past life regression, hypnotherapy, shamanism, and dowsing. Pamela has a graduate degree in anthropology, undergraduate degrees in archaeology and religion, and a 30-year career in social and biostatistical sciences. pamelanance.com.

ALISA M. PARCELLS is a life-long learner, poet, English teacher, and a holistic and healing arts practitioner with a passion for light, art and nature. She lives in Connecticut.

CHRISTINE PATTON is a transformational speaker, trainer, coach, and author who cares deeply about the health and happiness of the collective. Empowerment, resilience, and passion are the focal points of her work.

CORNELIA POWELL grew up on a farm exploring wonder, worked in fashion exploring dreams, spiritual journeyed the world exploring herself, and now lives on a green mountain ridge exploring more wonder. That wondering led her to connect with a 'mutual awakening' global community exploring new evolutionary possibilities for unity and relatedness. corneliapowell.com.

EFRAT SHOKEF, PH.D. is a mother, writer, and shamanic energy healing practitioner serving mainly spiritually aware children, teens, parents, and families.

CYNDAE CERRIDWYN STEPHENS has been writing since childhood, gestating stories for eons. The time to birth these stories has dawned. She holds space as an energy healer, soul-based coach, and communications muse.

JULIE SUEN, LLM., J.D., is an estate planning lawyer, TEDx speaker, Ascension guide, author, and podcast host. She guides awakening souls through transitions—whether it's one's own physical death, passing of a loved one, or spiritual ascension. She also supports starseeds in embodying their higher purpose. juliesuen.com.

JOANNE WARFIELD is a spiritual pilgrim weaving from gallerist back to art photographer and author of the photo memoir *Modern Nomad, Into The Heart Of The Silk Road, Afghanistan 1977.*

HELLEVI E. WOODMAN is an entertainer, yogi, author, speaker, and medicine woman. She is a passionate explorer of earth's magical mysteries and practical sacred tools for conscious being, dreaming, and dying.

MEET THE AUTHOR

Freddy Silva is a bestselling author, and leading researcher of ancient civilizations, restricted history, sacred sites and their interaction with consciousness. He is also the leading expert on crop circles. He has published eight books in six languages and produced fourteen documentaries.

Described by one CEO as "perhaps the best metaphysical speaker in the world right now," he leads sell-out tours to sacred sites worldwide, and for two decades he has been an international keynote speaker, with notable appearances at the International Science and Consciousness Conference, the International Society For The Study Of Subtle Energies & Energy Medicine, and the Association for Research and Enlightenment, in addition to appearances on Gaia TV, History Channel, BBC, and radio shows such as Earth Ancients, Fade To Black and Coast To Coast.

OTHER PUBLISHED WORKS:

The Divine Blueprint:
Temples, Power Places and the Global Plan to Shape the Human Soul

The Missing Lands:
Uncovering Earth's Pre-flood Civilization

Scotland's Hidden Sacred Past

The Lost Art of Resurrection:
Initiation, Secret Chambers, and the Quest for the Otherworld

Chartres Cathedral:
The Hidden or Heretic Guide

Secrets in the Fields:
The Science and Mysticism of Crop Circles

First Templar Nation:
How the Knights Templar Created Europe's
First Nation-state and a Refuge for the Grail

What I Learned from a Dog

Learn more at invisibletemple.com.

Made in the USA
Coppell, TX
23 July 2025

52246079R00132